Praise for Picasso's

A searingly honest account of Mallory's re
Pablo's son, as well as a wonderful journey
— — — — — — — Terry Jones, Monty Python

Carole Mallory seems to have crossed paths with just about every major figure in the art and entertainment world of the 1970s. Her new book brings you into the homes, yachts and bedrooms of everyone from Richard Gere and Robert DeNiro to Princess Grace and Peter Sellers with amazing recall and unabashed honesty she will make you feel you were there with her
— — — — — — —Patricia Resnick, screenwriter of 9 to 5 and A Wedding. Librettist of 9to 5 The Musical.

Carole Mallory is a born writer—funny, irreverent, often moving. Picasso's Ghost is an eminently readable romp with the Picasso family and the stars. But it's more—a poignant story of celebrity, love, and loss.
— — — — — — —Mary Dearborn, author of Mailer, and Mistress of Modernism: A Life of Peggy Guggenheim

A captivating, utterly intoxicating tour through late 1970s Hollywood and New York City, Picasso's Ghost captures an era and a spirit with effortless style and, better still, an emotional heft that lingers.
— — — — — —Megan Abbott, Edgar-award-winning author of Bury Me Deep, and Dare Me.

"Bold and moving. Mallory recounts, with disquieting directness, her long and emotionally complex romance with Claude Picasso. This is the story of a great love affair that haunts you long after you've finished reading it."
— — — — — — —Best-selling author Paul Alexander

"Addictive. Stunning indiscretions. Mallory creates an empathetic portrait of Pablo Picasso. By revealing historic, well-guarded secrets, Mallory could have solved the decades old mystery of why Picasso exiled Françoise Gilot, Paloma and Claude Picasso from The Great Master's life.
— — — — — — — — John Hancock, Director of Bang the Drum Slowly, and Weeds.

Carole Mallory's Picasso's Ghost is an amazing journey through the twisted soul of the late seventies, spanning Europe, New York City and Hollywood as well as the worlds of art, movies and advertising. Combining the best elements of the Hollywood memoir, the erotic autobiography and the recovery narrative. It's pure pleasure from start to finish."
— — — — — — — — —Scott Phillips, Winner, California Book Award for The Ice Harvest (also a film); The Walkaway, Cottonwood, and The Adjustment.

Peter Sellers, a magnificent clown, did Being There, a study of such gentleness, which Mallory captures in her memoir.
	---------George Kennedy, Oscar winning author of Trust Me.

Carole Mallory's wry wit and dry sense of humor keep the reader chuckling and head wagging until the very last page. Her keen sense of observation is unflawed as she dissects her global love affairs with the rich and famous icons of our time.
	-------*Sharmagne Leland-St. John, Five Time Pushcart Nominee for Poetry in books such as La Kalima; and co-author of Designing Movies: Portrait of a Hollywood Artist.*

Picasso's Ghost

A LOVE STORY

CAROLE MALLORY

Copyright ©2012 Carole Mallory
All rights reserved.

ISBN-10: 1479341851
ISBN-13: 9781479341856

Cover photo of Peter Sellers taken by the Author
Cover photo of Author with Dog taken by Peter Sellers
Drawing of Picasso by the Author

For My Father
Herbert Emile Wagner

Table of Contents

Picasso, Grace and Me 9
Claude and the family 23
Alone with Jackie O 37
Paris at Last 49
City of Lights 57
Death and Marriage 67
Rags (and Rejected) to Riches 79
Stepford Wife 89
Bohemian to Bourgeois 101
New York, My Kind of Town 109
Flying Over the Coo Coo's Nest 117
Taxi Driver 129
Inspecting Clouseau 135
Death and Dissolution 163
Goodbar Role 167
Mr. Goodbar 173
Malibu 183
War of the Wives 191
Dressed to Wed 197
Darkest Hour 207
Dawn and Beyond 221

Picasso, Grace and Me

"I want you both to meet Claude Picasso," Princess Diane Von Furstenberg said to my husband, Ron, and me. We were seated at a crowded table in the trendy discotheque Hippopotamus on New York's Upper East Side, a club owned by Richard Burton's wife, Sybil. It was the fall of 1971 and Diane was throwing a party.

Whenever Diane entertained, it was a lavish affair. In her sprawling Park Avenue co-op, decorated in wine-colored chintz, she threw catered dinner parties for the rich and famous. Waiters would take your drink orders. A buffet would be offered in the dining room, but the entire candle-lit apartment, even the bedrooms, would be filled with tables for guests. Giving a party in a discotheque was unusual for Diane.

This past summer Ron and I had separated, but we were now trying to repair our marriage.

When I looked into Claude Picasso's deep brown eyes, I wondered, "Why? Why did I meet this man now?" I knew I had fallen in love. Claude looked just like his father, Pablo Picasso, except he had hair--masses of black, straight, shoulder-length hair and like Pablo's, a receding hairline. He had thick Frank Zappa-like sideburns. His eyes were bolts of energy that captivated me with their magnetism.

Claude extended his hand. When I touched his flesh and looked into his eyes, I wanted him. Only him. There and then. Forevermore. He was danger. I knew. I had read about his tortured relationship with his father. Claude's love was surrounded by minefields of hate protecting his Andalusian heart. He would hurt, could hurt, but underneath that emotional barbed wire, I would learn, was the most tender man I would ever know—though he would hide his vulnerability in flash. Bright colors. Sideburns like Frank Zappa. A turquoise ring the size of a quarter, a purple rabbit skin coat.

"Do you want to dance?" Claude asked.

"Of course," I said. My husband didn't dance. Besides, he had heard Claude's last name. Ron and I were both impressed by fame. But it was Claude's bold good looks that first won me.

Claude was born Picasso's palette. His raw canvas. His living brush strokes. His father's defiance. The anger in *Guernica* was in Claude's eyes, anger because Pablo had rejected him all those years. Claude wore that defiance like a cloak.

We walked to the dance floor as Gloria Gaynor sang, "I Will Survive."

I looked over Claude's small but sexy body. His tight leather trousers and matching rose-colored T-shirt revealed every taut muscle. Claude didn't care how he looked. His passion was overwhelming. Spanish, after all.

And we danced. In my purple and red ankle-length dress, I followed Claude's lead. I felt like we were in a coliseum, the onlookers at the nearby cocktail tables spectators at the bull fight. I was the toreador and Claude was the bull. His buttocks proudly swayed with the rhythm. It was a fine ass. Beautiful. Firm. A Picasso ass. A defiant Spanish ass. In the years to come there would be nights when we would lie in bed and I would study the splendor of his naked buttocks.

And he was a great dancer. Passionate. He would embrace me in time with the music and then let me go, my skirt would fly in the air and my heart following. All eyes were on us. I didn't care. I liked the attention. I wanted witnesses to this moment. It was surreal. No, cubist! Things were askew. Nothing was as it should be. I had no guilt about being a married woman displaying my longing for Claude, sexual feeling I had repressed for too long, long-repressed longing as he drew me to him and smiled. He flashed his beautiful white teeth that cabled his pleasure in touching me. In front of everyone.

All his flash, rose leather pants, turquoise ring, purple rabbit skin coat, and references I would hear him make to Henry Miller and Celine, all the shits!, Merdes!, fucks! I would hear from him, hid the soft, tender, lost little boy I would come to love.

And we danced...

And I could feel us falling in love.

The music ended.

"Too soon," I said.

"You're a wonderful dancer," he said. "And so beautiful," he said. "Thanks, I needed this," he said.

Then Claude returned to his wife, and I returned to my husband.

That night I dreamed of Claude and his muscular body touching mine--when the body next to me was that of Ron Mallory.

Claude and Carole

Fantasies about Claude persisted. Ron went to Milan for a show of his recent sculpture and we decided to separate again.

Carole Mallory

Claude and Carole in Easthampton

I had been proud to marry Ron, an artist known for his hypnotic chemical art. David Rockefeller, the Whitney, the Nelson Aldrich Museum, and the Museum of Modern Art had all bought Mallory mercury sculptures. Mercury and jet engine oil were combined, then encased in plastic and mechanized. The movement of the mercury, which depended on the weather, descending through the oil was erotic. When the mercury fell into an air pocket, the effect was orgasmic.

Because of our friendships with other artists such as Rothko, Richard Lindner, Christo, and Andy Warhol, we had a modest art collection. Not only did he show his work at a well-connected gallery, talented Ron knew how to charm the rich, social, status-conscious collector, and sometimes he sold his sculptures directly to them. Marriage to Ron Mallory was fun, introducing me to a world I felt I would never have known without him.

Ron and I had sailed from St. Tropez to Capri on the *Black Swan*, a yacht once owned by Errol Flynn but now belonging to Felix Mechoulam. Felix, who made his millions selling brooms to Mexicans, treated my husband as his son, calling him "Ronaldito."

Picasso's Ghost

At Capri we stayed in Felix's villa, although he owned the Quississana Hotel where we dined on *langouste* and *fruits de mer*.

In Lake Worth, near Palm Beach, we had cocktails at the Lannan Museum, and dined at the home of its founder, Patrick Lannan, Sr., a collector of Ron's sculptures. Most people were afraid of billionaire Lannan's temper. I liked him. He was an elegant, good-looking man who liked to recite Dylan Thomas for his guests.

On the beaches of St. Tropez Ron and I had lunched with Bada Muller, the son of the King of Kuwait, whom Harold Robbins immortalized in his novel, *The Pirate*. Bada had invited me on a date, but I preferred the company of my husband, which created some tensions for Ron and me socially in St. Tropez.

As guests Ron and I had been invited to villas, on cruises and to castles in Italy and Spain. We vacationed during winters in Mégève and during summers in the south of France or Sardinia. At the King's Club of the Palace Hotel in St. Moritz we drank and danced with the Shah of Iran. In Manhattan we dined with Julie Christie and Warren Beatty who introduced himself to me at a party and propositioned me within a few sentences. "If you ever want me, just call the Carlyle," he said. "Some nerve," I thought, finding him both rude and conceited.

In Porto Cervo Ron and I were guests for a dinner at the Aga Khan's home where I spilled red wine on his white carpet, silently leaving the room and hoping I wouldn't get caught. We danced in discotheques in St. Tropez alongside Brigitte Bardot and partied there with Romy Schneider, Dominguin, Pierre Salinger, Allesandro Onassis, Spyros and Philip Niarchos, Roman Polanski, and Prince Juan Carlos De Bourbon of Spain, later the king.

Then one summer Ron and I were invited on a cruise with Austrian-born art collector Sam Spiegel, well-known for producing *Lawrence of Arabia* and *On the Waterfront*.

Sam had seen me on the beach of St. Tropez walking out of the water wearing only a black bikini bottom and a bullet belt slung on my hips, a look then all the rage. The beaches of St. Tropez were like cocktail parties. Screenwriter David Newman, who wrote *Bonnie and Clyde*, introduced us to Sam and only minutes later Sam asked if we wanted to go on a cruise with him the next morning to Corsica.

"Be on board at 6 AM," Sam said sternly. "Don't be late or we'll leave without you."

Five days later, after meeting a witty and charming Kirk Douglas in the port of Cap Ferrat and dining with a quiet, sullen David Niven in Portofino, we found ourselves gazing at the splendor of the Corsican coastline while pondering what was billed as a surprise luncheon, speculating on the identity of the mystery guest.

"It's Princess Grace!" I said to my husband Ron about the woman who stepped out of the rubber raft wearing a battered straw hat, a one-piece suit, and red rubber flip-flops. "And there are Prince Rainier with Princess Caroline and Prince Albert." I peered through binoculars at the guests who boarding Sam's 110-foot yacht, the *Melahne*. Sam was producing *Nicholas and Alexandra* at the time and wanted Princess Grace to star as Alexandra. Sam had kept his rendezvous with the royal family a secret.

Though at the time middle-aged, Princess Grace was no less a beauty, even without makeup. She was natural both in appearance and in her unpretentious personality. I was wearing a white bikini, with the potential to spark jealousy in many women, but the princess seemed not to mind this, instead acting warm and gracious toward me.

Though he was not photogenic, close up and in person, Prince Rainier was handsome. When he spoke, he put on no airs. No pretensions. He was down to earth and aware of other people's feelings. I had the impression that besides being charming, he was kind.

Nervous about protocol, Sam did not seem to know how to seat his guests for the luncheon so Prince Rainier helped out by offering to sit by my side. Wine was poured in abundance. Sam wasn't the only one nervous, I thought, as I drank my first glass of white wine. During the lunch, I finished a bottle.

Princess Grace seemed intimidated by Sam and was quiet throughout the luncheon. I could tell by her aloof manner when she addressed Sam that she had no interest in returning to films.

"We almost capsized in the storm last night," Prince Rainier said to Sam. I wondered why their sailboat was only thirty feet in length.

"Glad you didn't," Sam said. "Have some filet mignon or fresh langouste."

There was a great deal of silence so, hoping to counteract the somber atmosphere, I asked Prince Rainier, "What sign are you?"

"Gemini. And you?" he asked with a half-smile.

"Capricorn, and I'm from Philadelphia," I said, smiling at Princess Grace, who let out a chuckle.

"I'm from Philadelphia, too," she said. "What part are you from?"

"Springfield, Delaware County," I said, staring into her beautiful eyes.

"I'm from Lower Merion. Thereabouts," she said, in her lilting voice.

"I used to teach school there. Art to 7th graders. Welsh Valley."

"I know it well. Sam, it's good to see you have some culture and education on board besides the film industry."

Sam's eyes glistened. He rarely smiled. He had been raging for the entire cruise until we met the royal couple. I knew his temper masked his fear of disapproval. I wanted Her Serene Highness and His Serene Highness to like me, too. That was part of the reason I drank.

After lunch we all retired to the top deck. Rather tipsy from the wine, I lay for a few minutes trying to sunbathe. Then we all began discussing exercise. Prince Albert was doing push-ups on a mat in front of us. In an attempt to join in, I found myself doing push-ups at Princess Grace's feet when I fell on my face.

"*Je suis mal élève*," I said which meant, "I am badly raised."

Princess Grace laughed at my bad pun and for a moment I felt the closeness I longed for from a sister.

Carole Mallory

Prince Rainier's letter to Carole who in 1968 met Princess Grace.

March 17, 1983

Dear Mrs. Mallory:

      I am certainly very appreciative of your kind letter of March 5, in which you recall the very enjoyable times we all had aboard Mr. Spiegel's yacht several years ago.

      Let me express my sincere thanks to you for your kind prayers and for your comforting words of sympathy on the sad occasion of my beloved wife's death.

      My children join in expressing our heartfelt gratitude.

      Most sincerely,

Mrs. Carole Mallory
1216 North La Cienega
Los Angeles, California
United States of America

A letter from Prince Rainier to me upon Princess Grace's death

Picasso's Ghost

When the royal family left, sadness overcame the *Melahne*. Sam's dark mood returned as our vessel sailed back to St. Tropez. But Ron and I would never forget those few hours.

When Princess Grace died, I wrote Prince Rainier with my condolences. In a letter in return he expressed his gratitude for my having written and fondly remembered our cruise.

Each winter when Ron Mallory and I returned to our one-bedroom apartment in Manhattan, we entertained a lot of the rich and famous, and Ron seemed to think that I was a great hostess to some of these people. Before each dinner party I would clean the wineglasses with Windex.

Despite our glamorous lifestyle, there was hollowness to it all. I felt a lack of purpose. Unfulfilled. Because I felt inferior to these celebrities, I developed the habit of drinking heavily in their presence. In the fall of 1971, I realized part of the problem was that I no longer loved Ron. By the time I met Claude, I knew I wanted a divorce.

Carole and Claude Easthampton

Feeling unable to deal with being a single woman in New York, terrified of dating and feeling lost without Ron, I threw myself back into my modeling and acting classes. My teacher was Wyn Handman, the director of the American Place Theatre. In Wyn's absence, Tony Perkins, known for his performance in *Psycho*, taught the class, and Tony's wife, Berry Berenson, was a classmate. We did scenes from *Hedda Gabler* and *Streetcar*. Richard Gere, Brad Davis, Marisa Berenson, Phillip Anglim, and Penny Milford were some of my other classmates besides my friend, Heather MacRae who was starring in *Hair* on Broadway.

Later, Heather invited me backstage at *Saturday Night Live*. She was good friends with Edie Baskin, the Baskin Robbins heiress who was the photographer for *SNL*. Edie and I had modeled together, and her mother, the art collector Shirley Baskin, had bought my husband's sculptures. When Rod Stewart was a guest on *SNL*, Edie took a photograph of the two of us.

Rod Stewart and me at SNL

18

Picasso's Ghost

In 1971 Edie invited Heather and me to *SNL* after parties where I met John Belushi, Dudley Moore, Chevy Chase, Buck Henry and various guest celebrity hosts. We would drop in at producer Lorne Michael's apartment in the haunted Osborne on West 57th Street, near Carnegie Hall, and hang around until 3 or 4 AM. John Belushi would entertain us by doing monologues and characters with funny accents. I would listen and I would drink. Most of us did drugs and drank, except for Lorne Michaels and Buck Henry. One night Dudley put me in a taxi about 4 AM, making it clear he wanted to come home with me. While Ron and I were separated and had agreed to date other people, I did not respond to Dudley's advances, as I was by then obsessed with Claude.

Dudley Moore and me

Not long after this I went to a party for the film *A Safe Place*, and met Abbie Hoffman. He was adorable. We were about to get into a cab when his wife, Anita, yelled, "She's too straight for you, Abbie." Abbie changed his mind and said goodbye to me at the curb.

Many a night I would lull myself to sleep with a bottle of wine and a Valium. I was lonely. The thought of Claude haunted me.

19

Carole Mallory

Carole and Claude romancing

One day I called my modeling agency, and asked to be sent on a go-see to Claude Picasso, whom I knew worked as a photographer. A go-see was a meeting with a client or photographer during which the model introduced herself and showed her photos.

"You're not his type," the head booker said, and refused to send me to see him.

Claude was photographing mostly stills of products.

While that March I had been on the covers of *Newsweek*, *Cosmopolitan*, and *New York Magazine*, I did not like the way my agency was treating me. Maybe they were trying to protect me from him, I wondered. Did he have a reputation for trying to have sex with models? Later Claude confessed that to make ends meet he assisted in directing porno films, but this was unknown to my agency. I never did learn the real reason my agency would not send me to meet Claude again, but fate had other ideas in any case.

Picasso's Ghost

Claude and His Family

One snowy night on my way to acting class a few months later, I rounded a corner by Carnegie Hall and bumped into Claude Picasso.

"Claude, it's Mrs. Ronald Mallory," I said.

"I know," he said, laughing. A tear fell from his eye onto his purple rabbitskin coat.

I thought his tear was for me. (He had conjunctivitis).

"I'm getting a divorce," I said, smiling.

"So am I," he said, smiling. "Want to have dinner tomorrow?"

"Sure."

"I'm late for Jacques Brel's concert. Could I have your number? You're not listed."

"True," I said, jotting my number onto a slip of paper he had handed me. "My acting class has started."

"À demain," he said, kissing both my cheeks. I felt his tear and remembered those lips. So Claude had tried to find me while I had been trying to find him. My heart raced.

Moments later in my acting class, Richard Gere did a scene with Brad Davis. While their sexuality was exciting, nothing turned me on more than thoughts of Claude.

My favorite photo of Claude

The next evening Claude arrived with a dozen white daisies.

"For you, Chérie," he said, handing me the flowers and kissing me on both cheeks. As he walked into my living room, he studied my art collection, which must have seemed foolish to the son of the world's greatest artist, and then sat on my leather sofa. "You like Italian design, I see."

"I invested my savings from modeling into designer furniture and that Chryssa," I said, referring to my blue neon sculpture in front of the terrace. I opened a bottle of wine as Claude turned the mercury sculpture on the cocktail table on its side.

"That's by Ron," I said, sitting by Claude's side as I poured the wine.

"I like it and your Chryssa. Neon sculptures are hot in the art market right now. Here's to us," he said, making a toast. Then he put the glass down and took me in his arms. We kissed for the first time. I never wanted his lips to leave mine. It was that kind of kiss. His lips were full, comforting—yet determined.

Within minutes we were in the bedroom. As he undressed, I studied his muscular body. Claude was the photographer, but I would love to photograph him. He was small, and though his legs were short, his torso was perfect. His skin felt smooth, like the finest French silk. He even smelled French with a slight scent of cigarettes, but to me this was not offensive. His hair fell disheveled onto his shoulders which added to his desirability. His voice could be high when he was nervous, but normally it was well placed and had a cheerful resonance. He had a slight stutter that I later realized had stemmed from Picasso's abuse.

As he held me, he said, "Je vais ouvrir ta boutique." This became a game we played between us each time we made love. Claude would open up the boutique between my legs with his hands and his gaze. He had incredible control over his muscles. He used his short legs to his advantage, wrapping them around my waist and moving rhythmically and forcefully inside me. Claude loved to have control over me. In the beginning I didn't mind being controlled by him. I wanted to give him pleasure. Anything that would make him smile. He was so sad, I would learn. He suffered from such a sense of loss. It was as though he were an orphan because his father would not recognize his existence.

But it was the hypnotic gaze from his dark penetrating eyes that controlled me. Forget "Bette Davis eyes." Claude had "Picasso eyes." The magnetism that leapt from them would put me under Claude's spell for many years to come.

We didn't leave my apartment for several days.

Claude moved in immediately. In the beginning of our love affair I didn't question this. I felt lost without Ron Mallory, who had organized my social life. My life, period. I longed for companionship and was drinking alone at night. Though Claude's move was sudden, it was welcomed. He seemed as lost as I was, and in 1971 we were a perfect fit.

His wife, Sara Schulz Picasso, had kept their apartment. Claude had been living with a friend who was helping him develop his career as a photojournalist.

After a long day modeling, I liked to have dinner by candlelight in bed. Claude loved to cook. His specialty, *lapin*. One night, over one of his first gourmet feasts, we recalled the evening we met.

"I thought a lot about you since that night," he said. "Didn't know how to reach you and had to work out my feelings for Sara. Now we're divorcing for sure."

"It's hard to let go of Ron."

"I can tell," he said, laughing. "'Mrs. Ronald Mallory,' she says. Well, skooby do!

Dancing with you wasn't exactly an event I could forget, Chérie." Claude pinched my chin with his thumb and forefinger.

"I dreamed about you."

"Wet dreams, I hope." Claude squeezed my waist. "Mind if I read something by my favorite author? Kind of describes the way I felt outside of Carnegie Hall. You know, when I looked in your eyes and saw turquoise and quicksilver."

"Slow silver is more like it."

Claude laughed. "POW. Two smacks right in the kisser for that one."

"If I wear green, my eyes are green."

"If you're jealous?" Claude asked, tweaking my ear lobe.

"They're blue. I don't get jealous. So there. Read to me. Please?"

I snuggled next to Claude who reached for his jeans. Out of a pocket he pulled a folded piece of paper. "Blows your mind to read someone's thoughts just like yours, but you wanted to keep yours a secret. Then you think, 'Paff! What the fuck! Tell her.' So here's Henry." Claude caressed me as he read, "You walk away. I can't even move. I try to look and see where you're going, but my eyes are so blurred by the cold that you disappear in the night, out of reach. I am standing here not even knowing why."

"Who wrote that?"

"Henry Miller. Know him?"

"His work, not him," I said, not want wanting Claude to know that I'd read only one of his books.

"Henry's a friend. One day I'll introduce you to him and his wife, Hoki. She's Japanese. You'll like them."

"I like Henry Miller. I love you," I said, taking the paper out of his hand and blowing out the candles.

While we were together, I was busy modeling and doing print assignments for
clients such as De Beers, Revlon, Fabergé, and filming television commercials for Chevrolet, Almay, Clairol, and the like, which meant I had to get up at 5 AM to be on the set and wouldn't be finished until about 6 PM. Being a successful model was hard work.

Picasso's Ghost

Claude's career as a photojournalist had been a struggle to get assignments from the *Saturday Review*, *Brides* magazine and *Vogue*. Shortly after we met, he had a show of his photographs in New York. It illustrated a fantasy of his. The photos were of a redheaded woman with freckles all over her naked, childlike body. She was surrounded by dwarves and a stuffed bird with a huge beak. The critical reception was lukewarm.

Claude had worked for a while as an assistant for Richard Avedon.

"Photography was very easy," Claude told me. "I had immediate results, satisfaction. I felt like I was somebody. I was a photographer."

When Claude photographed me, the pictures were good, and I put them in my modeling portfolio along with my magazine covers. I felt they were worthy of inclusion with the photos of the top photographers for whom I had worked.

"Why did Avedon hire you?" I asked one day.

"I'm not really sure. When we met, we went to a coffee shop and he said I was getting to a very nice place with him. 'You will have to work very hard,' he said."

"I said, 'I didn't come here on holiday.'"

"Then Avedon said, 'We are all friends in this studio. I want you to be on the photography set with the models and magazine editors so that you learn. You can say anything you want. We all discuss everything.'"

"So I said, 'Cool. That really sounds incredible.'"

"I went on the set the first day. There was a *Vogue* shoot. I said, 'Could I look through the camera?'"

"I looked and said, 'Hey, man, that's no good.'"

"Avedon called up the studio manager and said to get me off the set. I was thrown off the set. I never got out of the darkroom again.

"Avedon was pissed because the minute I came in I showed him photographs of his that were printed like shit. Then I showed him photographs of mine that were absolutely incredible. Then I had to relearn everything, but it destroyed me to have to learn the technique. I was fucked up with technique. I was always thinking

'Aaaah, what am I going to do?' Then once I overcame the technique and assimilated it, I was free and just pssssst--I'd take pictures."

"Now photography's not enough. You don't say enough with a photograph. You say a lot of nice little thingies, but I have a lot to talk about. I'd like to express myself more elaborately."

Claude had a problem with humility, and he was insecure. He was always trying to overcompensate.

One night after Claude and I had been together a few months and he was in France, I had dinner with Mike Mangano, an art director with the prestigious advertising agency, Doyle, Dane and Bernbach. Mike had employed Claude to assist him filming commercials. Mike recalled the shock and amazement he felt when he learned Claude's last name. Claude had been working as a gofer, fetching various items needed for a shoot, doing odd jobs, and generally running around like an errand boy. Mike couldn't understand why Claude was doing this kind of work.

Since Claude was the son of a genius, Mike told me, he couldn't believe that he was doing something so menial and uncreative. Unfortunately Mike expected Claude to be artistic as did most of the world and foremost Claude himself. Claude was haunted by the need to compete with his father or live up to people's expectations

I understood Claude's difficulty getting work. I knew a lot of it had to do with his last name and how people liked to test him and even humiliate him because they resented his fame. At least this was how Claude viewed his troubled work history. People were constantly comparing him to his father. Mike Mangano had also expressed his surprise that Claude was so poor with such a rich father. I looked the other way and supported us.

After my marriage to Ron, I was used to this role. Ron needed money to buy mercury and other expensive supplies for his art. As I believed in his talent and his art, I had earned the money in that relationship as well. In 1972 Ron and I divorced.

While Claude himself was without money, his mother was wealthy, but only gave him a few hundred a month to live on. But maybe it was Picasso who gave him this money. I never learned where the monthly check came from and didn't care. I loved Claude, and I had to support him if I wanted him in my life. He had no home.

Claude had been staying with a friend, Bob Cato, who was in the music business and who would try to give Claude assignments. Cato kept the few pieces of furniture Claude owned when Claude moved in with me. Claude seemed too depressed to keep a steady job. I felt sorry for him and loved him despite his situation. I would dream of a day when maybe everything would be OK.

Never did I think he would see any of his father's money. A law called the Napoleonic Code stated that illegitimate children could not inherit an estate in the absence of a will. Everyone knew Picasso would not leave a will because he was superstitious and felt the drafting of one would bring on his death. So the Napoleonic Code would almost certainly block Claude from inheriting his father's wealth.

To make up for Claude's inability to pay the rent, he helped around the house. But I had a maid, Andre Rose Napoleon. Andre Rose spoke French, so Claude and Andre Rose became friends. She was from Haiti or "Ahitian," which was how "Haitian" was pronounced. When I came home exhausted after a shoot, I knew Claude or Andre Rose would have dinner ready, which was always comforting. I began to think of Claude as my "househusband." When my ex-husband suddenly moved to Berkeley to teach, he left his clothing behind. Claude wore Ron's clothes as he did not have much of a wardrobe . When pieces of my clothing fit Claude, I offered them to him. My Romanian blouse, which I wore on the cover of *Newsweek* became one of Claude's favorite shirts.

During a trip to La Jolla to meet Claude's mother, Françoise Gilot, and his stepfather, Dr. Jonas Salk, Claude did introduce me to Henry Miller. In 1972, Henry was quite wrinkled and nearly bald; what hair remained was white. His ears jutted out radically but his eyes still glistened as though he had a secret. He lived in Los Angeles with Hoki and her girlfriend who owned a boutique together. I was under the impression they all lived together. Hoki was not kind to Henry, and it was apparent that they were not having sex. We visited his home and saw her Japanese women friends surrounding Henry and fawning over him while behind his back they were on the phone ordering this and that while charging it to him. He seemed to want the attention of these women, who appeared to be freeloaders. After the local liquor store made a delivery these women ignored him. I felt sad for Henry, who was kind. He appeared to be hoping that Hoki would be the geisha of his fantasies when in fact she was duplicitous, using Henry for all she could get out of him. In 1977, they would divorce.

The Japanese fascinated Claude, who had many friends in Tokyo. His ex-wife had lived in Japan. Some part of Claude was very much like the Japanese. Quiet. Furtive. Shrewd. Rarely could I tell what he was thinking. An avid reader, he loved a good literary argument among friends. The topic was often Norman Mailer. Though Claude preferred Miller to Mailer, he enjoyed comparing their work and their intellects. "For me Mailer's best was *Armies of the Night*," Claude said. "But his writing suffers from blowhardness. Pontificating. Miller doesn't do this. Mailer was free of posturing in *Executioner's Song*."

Another writer Claude worshipped was Ferdinand Céline. Though Claude had learned English at Cambridge University, his manner of speech was more influenced by Céline's casual

gutter French. Words such as "paff," "zap," pow," and "zip" sounded interesting in his formal Cambridge accent. When Claude spoke, I thought I was listening to a cartoon come alive—a British Superman. Looking at Claude with his shoulder-length black hair and his small, muscular torso, so much like Pablo's, I was reminded of a Mexican mural painted by Diego Rivera. I would tease him about this, telling him he looked like a Mexican pea picker. I called him *"mon petit Mexican."* He would laugh and would call me, *"ma petite langouste."* (After living in my apartment for one year, my superintendent tried to throw Claude out. My super, who called Claude "Picaztzo," thought Claude was Mexican and an illegal alien.)

How others viewed Claude did not bother me. I loved looking at him, caring for him, and making a home with him. We were invited to many dinner parties, but unlike my ex-husband Ron who thrived on a robust social life, Claude refused these invitations. "When you can't afford to buy a Picasso, you invite one to dinner," he would say with a frown.

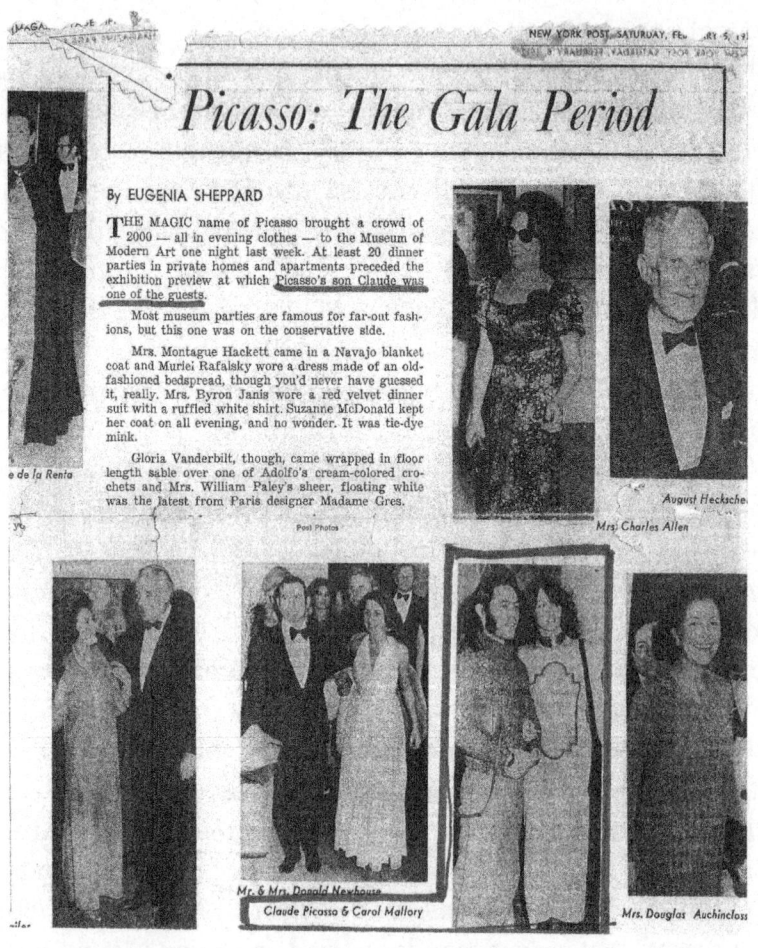

Claude never called Françoise Gilot "mother." She was always Françoise to him. Dr. Jonas Salk was Jonas to everyone. I grew fond of Jonas who was a bit like the absentminded professor. A kind and loving man.

I first met Françoise and her husband at their home in La Jolla, which was decorated in Danish modern and had a formal air to it.

"Carole, it's a pleasure to meet you," Françoise said. At 51, she was stunning with those famous circumflex eyebrows that fascinated not only Picasso but Matisse. Age had not made her less of the beauty Picasso immortalized. "Claude has told us so much about you," she said. Her voice was high and thin. There was a fragility to it that masked her strength of character. She wore no makeup. She had alabaster skin and the posture of a prima ballerina.

"Thank you for inviting me," I said as I sat down on the sofa. The home was so neat that I was afraid I would spill the glass of wine that Claude had given me.

Dr. Jonas Salk walked into the living room and joined us. "Hello, I'm Jonas," he said, stiffly extending his hand. When he spoke, it was as though something might break if he did not say exactly the right thing. He didn't drink alcohol, but Françoise, Claude, and I did. With his closely cropped grey hair and tortoise shell glasses Jonas exuded elegance and a restrained charm. He was deferential to Françoise, and I had the feeling that he viewed her as his living work of art.

"I hear you have a busy schedule modeling?" Françoise said.

"Some of the time. It can be stressful." I said, sipping my wine.

"I try to take care of you, Chérie," Claude said. He was seated next to me on the sofa and put his arm around me. "Carole likes my cooking."

"And your photography," I added.

"While you are here, I hope we can go for a drive up the coast toward Santa Barbara. Would you like that, Carole?" Françoise asked.

"I've never been. That would be fun." I said, eager to please.

"There's a Danish village along the coast which is a delight to visit. Do you agree, Claude?"

"Good idea, Françoise." Claude raised his glass of wine and toasted his mother.

The following day we set out for our journey, just the three of us. Jonas chose to stay behind to work at his nearby Salk Institute.

As we got into their car, Françoise asked, "Carole, do you mind if I sit in the front next to Claude? I have a back problem."

"Of course not," I said.

I sat in the back for the three-hour drive. This pleased Claude, who drove with great delight, happy to have his mother by his side. They talked to each other exclusively for long periods of time. I felt left out of the conversation. When we stopped for dinner at the restaurant Scandia in Beverly Hills, Claude toasted Françoise, who maintained eye contact with him as she toasted him in return with her Aquavit.

Later that night I said to Claude, "Why did your mother insist on sitting next to you for that long ride?"

"Oh, she says it's her back, but I know she confuses me with Pablo. It's been like that for I don't know how long. Paloma's the same way. It's because I look so much like him. Françoise is always telling me of her attraction to me. It's definitely weird, but I just accept it."

Alone with Jackie O

Pablo Picasso had exiled his son, Claude, from his life when Claude was a young teenager. In 1960, in an attempt to see his father, who'd become reclusive, Claude scaled the gates of his father's villa, Notre Dames des Villes outside of Cannes. Picasso set his dogs on his own son, and later tried to have him arrested. Pablo Picasso's behavior seems to have stemmed from his anger toward Claude's mother, who had not only walked out on the Great Master but had written a book about him, *Life with Picasso*. (Françoise was never legally married to Pablo.) Claude was haunted by the existence of a father who was alive but not emotionally present for him.

So was I. When I was 13, my father was needlessly given a lobot omy. During the operation the doctors discovered he had been suffering from Parkinson's disease. The lobotomy created permanent brain damage. The doctors apologized for their mistake; nevertheless, they still billed my mother. "Let those butchers try to collect," Mother would say. I admired her courage, but wondered why she never sued the doctor and the hospital.

Claude was kind to my father, who was reduced to half the man he was before the operation. As mentally ill as my father had become, the doctors had been unable to lobotomize his sense of humor.

"He's the only father ya got," Claude would say, smiling. Once my father and I visited the Bronx Zoo, and he and I got separated.

I called Claude to ask him what to do. Claude jumped in a cab in Manhattan, came to the zoo and found my father. People often belittled my father, who had developed a severe twitch and eye tics, and walked hunched over in a shuffle, one shoulder higher than the other. Claude never ridiculed my father's appearance. He treated my father with respect, just as if he were normal.

"Everyone wants to compare their father to my father," Claude would say with contempt, protecting Picasso despite the cruelty his father had inflicted upon him. In Claude's imagination he assumed the role of Pablo's father. This enabled him to forgive Pablo, whom he reduced to being a self-centered child, not a grown man responsible for Claude's pain and suffering. If Claude viewed his father as a self-obsessed child or a "big bad kid"—which was how he referred to Picasso—Claude could convince himself that his father's sadistic behavior was unintentional. Claude could love Pablo along with the rest of the world and not feel the outcast and unwanted son that he was.

More and more, Claude came to assume the role of a caretaker. He was good at it. I allowed him to care for my wounded sense of self. I blamed myself for my father's suffering.

After we had been living together about a year, Claude began making trips to Paris for photographic assignments. He liked to visit his grandmother in the wealthy Paris suburb of Neuilly. Everyone loved Grandmère, Françoise Gilot's mother, who in her 70s rode a motor bike.

Fortunately, Claude wrote and called me often. I felt abandoned and panicky when he left me. Because of this, and for a lot of complicated other reasons, I decided to accept dates with other men while he was gone. Shortly after I made this decision, the phone rang and it was Claude.

"How's *mon petite chou*?" he asked in a husky voice.

"Lonely."

"I'm coming home soon. Almost a year ago we met on a frozen corner and look where we are now."

"Right. You're in Paris and I'm in New York minding the store."

"You know I have to be here. I called to tell you that I'm happier than I've ever been, my darling, because I have the deepest relationship with you. Deeper than I've had with anyone in my entire life."

"If it's so deep, why didn't you take me with you? I don't like when you leave me, Claude. I feel like I'm your hotel."

"My hotel! Ah, common. Then I'm your houseboy. I'm here for two weeks. *Basta!* Meeting you has changed my life. I have to adjust. I never planned to stay in N.Y. I want to grow more in love with you and can't do that unless I feel free. Not free to fuck around. Really free to think that we love each other. To believe it."

"You have to be away from me to feel free? Do I smother you?"

"Look, Chérie. Don't mother me. Don't fence me in! I need space. You're turning two weeks into something out of *Dr. Zhivago*. It's no big deal."

"To you, obviously, but I don't know how to feel. What am I to do? Am I to sit here, watch TV, and feel free to love you? While you do exactly as you please without telling me what you are doing? Or asking me to join you? This is servitude, not a relationship."

Claude laughed. I didn't.

"Carolette, why are you making my coming to Paris a test of the strength of our love?"

"Because it is almost our anniversary and for practically one year I've been paying the rent. You borrow my parents' car, wear my clothing and my ex-husband's and then waltz off to Paris alone to stay with your rich grandmother to take care of you." Later, I realized Claude saved money by staying with family, but that night I ignored this in my rage.

Modeling would not support me for the rest of my life. My looks would not last forever. I had to think of my savings. Claude had no hope for a future income. My mother raised me to feel I was nothing without a man. The man was supposed to be the security in the marriage. Before my father's operation he had held three jobs to support our family. Claude was unable even to help pay the rent. Whatever money he did earn, he needed for his expenses. When I drank, I especially worried about money. Drinking and fear went together. Still I felt I had to drink when I was alone to help with my depression.

"This is not the time or place for such an argument. I have come here alone precisely because of work."

"What work?"

"A story on Jonas. He's here, you know. Those parasites at the magazine want me to pick the brain mind of Sabin, the other polio man, to get background for a story about Jonas. So, lovey, I'm having a tough time not talking about that and still making people understand that Jonas's way was prefect...without showing that I might be biased."

"Why didn't you tell me about the piece?"

"I didn't want to tell you about it because sometimes these stories don't work out."

"How's it going?"

"O.K. It's decent."

"Claude, I shot a campaign for Gordon's Gin with Bill King. I'm on billboards all over New York. I want you here with me. Come home?"

"I'm proud of you, Chérie. Bill King is the greatest photographer, but next week I've got to be in the south of France to photograph Chagall with his stained glass windows, which will blow their minds at *The Saturday Review*. Somebody's put up the loot for a museum down there. Should be fun to see Chagall. Been a long time."

I realized I had lost my argument. "How's Paloma?" I asked, trying to change the subject.

"In Greece making jewelry for Zolotas. Not for us, dearie. We'll never be able to buy a piece of her jewelry this year. $2,000 smackeroos a piece. The Antiquarian Fair's giving her an exhibit."

"So I guess you and your mother have stopped mocking her jewelry designs?"

"That was the past. She looks like she's on her way. No more ridiculing Paloma."

"Have you seen Andy Warhol or Fred Hughes?" I asked, referring to friends we shared. Fred took care of Andy and organized Andy's commitments. I'd met them both through my ex-husband.

Ron and Andy began their careers with the same gallery, the Stable Gallery. Ron thought Andy was mostly hype, but I respected him and his artwork. Ron and I had many a fight on the subject, but despite Andy's aloof manner I admired his keen wit and thought he was fun.

"Paloma's seen them. Fred told her he's taking a letter to you."

"When are you coming home?" I asked pouring a glass of wine.

"I told you, Chérie. I don't know for sure."

"Well, don't expect me to be sitting around knitting."

"Do as you like. Remember I love you and this trip is about work. And about this need I have to be alone and to get centered and feel free. Free to love you."

"Claude, I don't like your leaving me or your attitude toward commitment. You heard it here first." I downed the glass of wine and poured another.

Claude laughed. "I'm coming home soon. Faster then you can say 'Jack Robinson.' I miss you, twinkling turquoise in quicksilver."

"I miss your *zizi*."

"*Quel betesse sur le telephone*."

"Je t'aime."

"Moi aussi."

Clique. I finished the bottle of wine, took a Valium and went to bed.

The next day I got a letter from Claude. "I have to be here longer if I am going to do a good job. If I do a good job and I'm happy, I'll work well and make lots of money and we will get married and have children and travel and so on and so forth. My head is so full it is bursting. I want you. I love you. I am crazy about you. Be yourself, be happy, loving, generous and forget about everything else. Be mine. I am yours. Look at me, sniff me, listen to me. Listen to my heart between the lines, my concern, my caring, my clumsy love. I am stopping here. I have lost track of myself in all this. I love you. Claude."

Now he was going to stay away longer. I didn't like this.

One morning, a week after I received his letter, and without calling to tell me, Claude returned. I didn't hear him turn his key in the lock. It was late October. Dragging his luggage into the bedroom, he collapsed onto the bed. He was unshaven. His hair uncombed. His eyes bloodshot from the flight.

Still half asleep, I poured him a cup of coffee from my breakfast tray. "What is this? I don't get a kiss?" I asked, crawling back under the satin covers.

"Someone must have had a good time," he said, sitting on the edge of the bed, drinking his coffee.

"Yep, watching a funny rerun of Dave Letterman."

"Chérie, you make me laugh. I thought you'd be with itsy-bitsy Beatty or some such Hollywoodsman," said Claude who pulled me into his arms and kissed me. I kissed him back.

I was filled with anger at myself for my intense feelings for him. I wished I could be cold like he was. Walk out the door one week and back in the next without a care, without liability, without guilt. He was living in a time warp. It was as though his life were on hold and he were waiting at the starting line for that gunshot, that signal to begin living. To begin a race toward what? That was the part that baffled me and worried me the most. Who was Claude under all his fancy heritage and painterly past? If he were waiting to inherit his father's fortune, there was little hope. Picasso would not leave a will because he thought the signing of it would bring on his death. Many a night I had nightmares worrying about how we would survive. Claude didn't have steady clients or income. What would happen to us? I couldn't keep modeling forever.

"Tell me about Paris," I said, hoping to get out of my negativity.

Claude stretched out on the bed and held my head to his chest.

"I'll tell you everything so that you don't feel you missed out on anything. On the plane over here, there was Jackie Onassis and some friends. She even tried to check two beds the plane. Can you imagine? Two proper beds? There was a big fuss and that's why we were delayed."

I wanted to dodge any discussion about Jacqueline Onassis because I had made a date to go to a party for her wedding anniversary that very night and did not want to mention this to Claude yet. So I changed the subject. "How was Chagall?"

"He never showed up. I didn't have lunch or dinner. Just coffee and cookies on the auto route on the way there. It was a bum trip." Claude stared blankly at the ceiling." So I d-d-decided with time on my hands I'd try to see my father." Claude hadn't stuttered for several months.

"Did you see him?"

"Of course not. 'He's is out, Monsieur. There is no one home.' I've said this so many times to m-m-myself that it's absurd. I almost crashed through the gates of my father's villa because my stepmother's daughter drove u-up. She must be freaked, living this lie every day. That my father is buried alive. A corpse. My poor father is locked up in his d-dungeon alive. I love the old man. That's what makes me sad."

I held Claude, who looked pale and shaken,

"One day I know I'll r-replace him and take the role he never wanted, but that won't make up for the past." Claude paused for a moment. "The whole trip made me sick. It m-makes me think of that book *100 Years of Solitude*. The insanity of the Spanish people. I need you, my Carolina."

We held each other and began to make love when the phone rang, I didn't pick up the receiver, but let the machine answer. A voice said, "Hello, Carole, it's Mike. I'll be by at 8."

"Who's Mike?" Claude said, disturbed.

"Mike Nichols," I said, with hesitation.

"You have a date with Mike Nichols? Tonight?" Claude lit up a Gitane.

"Claude, I didn't know you were coming home. You didn't call, cable, or write. You appear like Houdini and expect me to be a welcome mat to be walked on."

"Chérie, tu exagére ... Excuse m-me." Claude stood up and put on his trousers. "What's on his schedule tonight besides you?"

"He's invited me to Jackie Onassis's anniversary at El Morocco."

"And you're going?"

"I'd like to. It's at El Morocco. I've never been," I said, not giv ing two hoots about El Morocco.

"Well, you worry about my cheating on you and I l-leave you alone for two weeks…"

"Two and a half."

"…and you're having a relationship with Mike Nichols." Claude took a deep drag on his cigarette.

"I've had dinner with him once or twice. Hardly a relationship."

"And now we've been to dinner twice with Monsieur Nichols. And where did we meet him?"

"Through my friend, Buck Henry…"

"And where did we meet Buck Henry?"

"Back stage at *Saturday Night Live* with Heather MacRae. Want to know where I met Heather?"

"No, thanks. I'm going to a walk," Claude said with a pasty grin. As he walked out of the apartment with his cigarette in hand, he slammed the door in my face.

I wondered what I was doing with my life. It wasn't right that Claude had treated me the way he had. He wasn't paying rent and had treated my apartment like a hotel that he felt he could skip out on any time day or night. Oh, maybe I was overreacting, but I wondered what he was waiting for? Why couldn't he as he would say, "get his shit together?" Why should I stop my life and wait for him to start his? No, I was going to keep my date and my experience. When we had been together, Mike Nichols, an Oscar, Tony and Emmy winning director, had treated me like a lady and with respect. I didn't think Claude Picasso had treated me with respect.

At about 7 PM Claude returned from his temper tantrum and went into the bedroom . At 8 PM Mike rang my doorbell and I greeted him while in the bedroom Claude sat quietly reading Celine's *Death on the Installment Plan*. Mike did not know Claude was in the bedroom.

I felt bad deceiving Mike and leaving Claude alone, but what was I to do? It was an awkward, uncomfortable situation. I wanted to meet Jacqueline Onassis and I felt special in Mike's company.

He made me laugh and I needed to laugh. My father's suffering haunted me. Though I loved Claude, our relationship was fraught with confusion and question marks. There were no substantial plans for the future or our well-being. Claude's inability to support me while he was around was one thing, but when he left and wanted me to stop leading my life, I put my foot down. I was angry that he had not taken me to Paris to meet his grandmother. I was good enough for a love affair in America when I was paying for him, but not for one in Paris where his family was paying for him. Simple as that.

Mike and I immediately left in his limousine.

At 1 AM I returned home, said good night to Mike at the door and tiptoed into the bathroom. Claude, fully clothed, had not changed his position on the bed. However he was now reading *100 Years of Solitude*. I dodged confrontation as long as I could, then feigned indifference. I walked into the bedroom.

Claude continued to read.

"Haven't you read that book?" I asked.

"Only twice," Claude said.

"Well, it wasn't very special really," I said, referring to the party.

Claude put the book on the coffee table. "I won't leave you alone again, Chérie. You look beautiful and I'm glad you went. You have to get that stuff out of your system."

"She was very nice. Jacqueline Onassis. Really."

"Did you talk with her?"

"Shook her hand in the receiving line. Said hello. She flirted with Mike. I think they had a thing. She was lovely. Reminded me of a giant swan."

"How's that?" Claude said with a grin.

"So tall and yet graceful. I had the impression that she's very funny under all that etiquette. She probably has to distance herself and act a certain way because of her fame and childhood," I said, then realized that Claude's childhood with Picasso must have been more scarred by being hounded by press than was Jacqueline Bouvier's as a child.

"Did you meet Ari?"

Carole Mallory

> Mike Nichols & Carole at
> Anniversary Party for
> Jacqueline Onassis
> at El Morocco published
> in LIFE MAGAZINE
> about 1972

Jacqueline Onassis, Mike Nichols and me from *Life Magazine*

"Just shook his hand. They weren't together much during the cocktail hour. *Life* magazine took our picture though," I said, forgetting that Claude sometimes photographed for *Life*.

"You and Ari?" Claude said, laughing.

"Mike and I walking in," I said, ignoring his sarcasm.

(Jacqueline Onassis, Mike Nichols and me from Life Magazine)

"Thought you'd be back earlier."

"Mike wanted us to go back to the Beresford for a drink."

"What!" Claude slammed the book on the end table. "I've tried to be understanding, Cherie, but what the fuck were you doing? You went to his apartment?"

"We weren't alone."

"Oh, who chaperoned?" He sat up straight, arms folded.

"Jack Nicholson and his date."

"Oh, Jackie baby, well, la-de-da. Did Jackie know about your fling with his buddy, the itsy Beatty?"

"We didn't talk about such things."

"Bet they did."

"Claude, you're overreacting. I couldn't tell Mike what to do. To drop me off right after dinner. It wouldn't have been right."

"Keep on breaking my balls, Chérie, and one day the big balloon will blow up and there won't be a way to patch it up any way you try. I've taken enough abuse in my life and had my fill."

"Claude, don't ever leave me alone again," I said, sitting by his side.

"I won't. I promise," he said, wiping my tears.

"And take me to Paris."

"I'll never leave you again, my Carolina."

"Shall we open the boutique?" I asked.

"I think we should have a rummage sale, don't you?" Claude said, pulling me into his arms. Then we opened the boutique and made love.

Claude ravaged me, kissing with a passion he had not shown before. He pushed me down on the bed. "Let me see your beautiful mound of Venus, your big round cul," he said, smiling and placing his full thick lips on mine. He knew how to make me wet with his tongue and with his *bon mots*. He called me his *petite langoustina*. When we made love, he lowered his voice so that it had a timbre that resonated in my soul.

Claude was nurturing. He was loving. He was mine.

He now inserted his beautiful penis, which he called his zizi, deep within me and moved with a vigor that only a short man can have. I loved the way his short legs wrapped around my waist while he held me tightly in his grasp.

I imagined this was how Pablo Picasso had had sex with Françoise Gilot. Picasso was shorter than Claude and Françoise was shorter than me. But they must have had passionate sex for her to be so obsessed with him. His short legs and penetrating gaze must have captivated Françoise—besides his genius, of course. She was not an easy one to control, but in the bedroom Picasso must have had her under his spell.

When Claude and I made love, I often imagined that he was Picasso. Claude's cock was the closest I would ever get to Picasso. I loved this thought and the power that it gave me. Picasso's drawings contained one penis after the next. Unapologetic. Unabashed. The minotaur was power. The bull was a sexual symbol.

Claude made love like a bull. Like he was going to demolish me with the power of his stare, the power of his magical weapon, his *zizi*. I was the matador but I would fail at killing the bull. The bull would trample me.

And that's just what happened.

Paris at Last

Claude was proud of my modeling career. He liked to photograph me and enjoyed showing my magazine covers to his friends and to his family. His mother was also kind to me.

After Claude and I had been together for some time, Françoise said, "Here is something I want you to have for taking care of Claude and making him happy." She handed me an original piece of jewelry designed by Picasso. It was a tiny sculpture of a minotaur's head, the size of a silver dollar. Its horns curved outward like rounded asymmetrical hooks. Its thin nose, crudely formed, in profile resembled an erect penis. Its eyes, carved-out sockets with rings of metal for lids. Its mouth opened slightly into a crooked smile with a recessed indentation, which had no teeth or lips. A tiny ring rose above the minotaur's head where a ribbon or a chain could be inserted.

"This is too kind of you," I said, stunned.

Claude's gaze was blank though he put his arms around me and kissed me on my cheek.

I supposed this was Françoise's way of thanking me for giving Claude a home.

Immortalized in Pablo's many portraits, Françoise, who lacked vanity, enjoyed making fun of her beauty. On holidays around the staid community of La Jolla with her husband, Dr. Salk, by her side, she would wear green and purple wigs to neighbors' cocktail parties.

Deeply attached to his mother, Claude enjoyed playing the role of her caretaker as well.

She responded by asking his opinions and giving him a sense of importance, never hesitant to show her dependence on him, especially in decision-making.

I often felt in the way, but realized Claude needed Françoise more than most of us need our mothers because he had no father. I had to suppress my ego and my need for attention when Françoise was in the room. I was grateful Claude had Françoise to take care of him, just as she was grateful to me for the same thing.

One night shortly after he had returned from his trip to Paris Claude told me, "Françoise read my palms and said she could tell that I would become the head of the family. It's quite amusing since I told my analyst a long time ago that would probably be my destiny. I was my own father and her own father. Paloma, who thought the same about me as Françoise, was sexually attracted toward me and now my half brother, Paulo, is coming to me for my opinions. I attract this and welcome it. Obviously I relish the idea of replacing my father."

As helpless as Claude's mother could appear, she had the mind of a lawyer. "Her father wanted a boy and I guess her becoming an attorney was to please her father," Claude told me. Françoise had been beaten by her father when she left home to live with Picasso

Therefore Françoise, who was a writer and a painter, was driven by accomplishment. Using her legal knowledge, she sued the French government for Picasso's estate. Françoise had never married Picasso and her children were illegitimate. The Napoleonic Code stated that illegitimate children could not inherit if there were no will. Napoleon had many illegitimate children throughout Europe, but this was an antiquated, chauvinistic law that had to be abolished if Françoise's children were to get to any of Picasso's fortune upon his death. Françoise began her lawsuit to abolish the Napoleonic Code prior to Picasso's death. Claude would ridicule her about this, feeling that she was making a fool of him. In 1971 when we first met, Claude claimed he wanted no part of Picasso's fortune. Because he was deeply angry with his father, Claude said he did not want his father's money. Claude was defiant and proud and wanted to make his own money. His mother's trying to overturn the Napoleonic Code was such a legal challenge that Claude felt it was absurd of his mother to even try. He cared what people thought of him. He had felt inferior all of his life because of his father's fame. Unintentionally, Françoise was adding to his feelings of inferiority. *Enfin*, Claude feared his mother would make him look like a greedy son who had no love for his father and was only seeking the fortune of the rich Pablo Picasso, who was close to a national treasure in France.

Several months after Claude and I had been living together, he decided to paint the bedroom chartreuse and dyed the blankets a deep purple. *Fauve* colors were his favorites. That day I had filmed a Fabergé commercial.

Photo of me for Faberge Tigress

Because the paint was drying in the bedroom, where we usually ate, we dined by candlelight in the dining room. Claude had prepared *pot au feu*.

"So how was Mike Cimino's direction?" asked Claude, who wanted to be a director himself.

"Temperamental. We never met before the filming. Fabergé had cast me without him."

"That should have kept him in line."

"Not really. The first take he said, 'They told me you were sexy.' I began to cry and had to go back to makeup because my individual lashes, glued on one by one, fell off. Lost two hours of filming. Then he apologized and the commercial turned out fine."

"Fabergé like it?"

"Think so. All I know is that it is good to be home."

"Fabergé got their tigress." Claude rolled his eyes and looked at the ceiling. "You have a temper, Dearie."

"Mike was temperamental. I cried."

"We know your tears, *petite bébé*. They got you what you wanted, didn't they?" he said, pinching my cheek.

"I was hoping to get sympathy."

"I know you. Instead you're getting an airline ticket."

"To where?"

"Paris."

"Oh, my. Why?" I put my arms around Claude and sat on his lap.

"*Look* magazine wants me to photograph Dominque Sanda next week. She lives somewhere outside Paris with Christian Marquand."

"I'll be jealous."

"You won't."

"Yes, sir." I saluted Claude.

"There'll be ground rules. Instead of hearing you yak away on the phone because you don't know what to do, you'll relax. Not go shopping. Walk my dog in the Bois de Boulogne. Look at the boats. And come and smell an open market with me."

"Oui, Monsieur."

"And I can listen to you all day long."

"Does your grandmother know?"

"She wants to meet you."

"We'll go to the country?"

"We might drive to Aix en Provence and visit a tiny town called Paulette." Claude paused, "Did I tell you that my father bought the Mt. St. Victoire, the mountain Cezanne made famous? Unfortunately, he bought the wrong side." Claude chuckled.

"What's the wrong side?"

"The side of the mountain, the one not painted by Cezanne. It's over 3000 feet high and there's this big cross on top. From the road you see the countryside Cezanne loved. As you drive out of Paulette, on the left this mountain suddenly springs out. Something to see."

"Were Cezanne and your father close?"

"My father respected the eyes of Cezanne, but when I wanted my father's attention, I told him my favorite painter was Matisse."

"How'd your father like that?"

"Not much. That's why I did it." Claude grinned yet his eyes remained blank.

"Wouldn't it depress you to go back to Aix?"

"I'd like to see it again. The road's bordered with *souvenirs*. There were the restaurants we used to stop at, the antique shop, the petrol pump, the bend where we were arrested and where my father flashed his police commissioner's badge. Which was gold-plated and studded with rubies, diamonds and sapphires replacing the usual enamel. Crazy shit like that was lying all over the fucking place. It was funny."

Claude claimed he did not want to talk about his father, but he would repeat the same stories, always with that blank stare.

"They're happy memories," he said, "like the time the Russians paid my father a visit. He pulled his r-revolver on them and they shit in their pants. Then there was the sculpture of the goat that we used to piss on to give it patina."

Hoping to change the subject because I had heard these stories many times before, I said, "What should I pack?"

"What I'm proposing when I say come to Paris could be a dangerous step. You'll have to face me as I really am and face yourself in the situation you say you want to be in. You see if I take care of you, Chérie, you'll have to go along with me."

I could feel one of Claude's paternal lectures coming on.

"This could make life easier for you. Fewer decisions and responsibilities, but you may lose a certain freedom and independence that you're striving for. You're very important in my life and therefore a great source of worry. I need to spend some time by myself for work and quiet. You know, I dream of your being able to sit and read or draw portraits of my dog, Tutu. Besides you he is the love of my life and needs attention that you could give him while I can write. Instead of hearing you yak away on the phone because you don't know what else to do."

"You're repeating yourself, Claude."

"When I'm taking pictures, you'll have to be your own man."

"Woman, thank you," I said, clearing the table. When I had put all the dishes in the kitchen, I sat by Claude's side, held his hand and looked into his eyes. "Shall we see if the paint's dry in the bedroom?"

Claude didn't respond.

After a long uncomfortable silence I said, "Claude, stop putting me down or I won't go to Paris. I've had one fight with a director today. I don't want to fight with another. I want to make love to him. Ça va?"

"Ça va." Claude said, smiling mischievously as he picked me up and carried me into the chartreuse bedroom.

As he unzipped his jeans, I studied his muscular body. Despite his short legs, his torso was perfectly proportioned. His skin was smooth and a dark olive. He smelled like the countryside after a rain. When he was completely naked, I marveled at his enormous *zizi*. He had long black pubic hair that hung straight over his *rupettes*, as he liked to call them. I liked to comb this hair. It was that long. His jet-black pubic hair and his long straight black hair receding from his forehead made me wonder whether he had been a Japanese samurai in another life. His thick sensuous lips pressed protectively on mine. He took off my clothing with a passion I had only seen in movies.

"Let's get rid of these *vêtements*," he said in a whisper as he pulled my sweater over my head. I never wore a bra so that he could get to my breasts quickly. He loved to talk to them and to put his head between them. "Let me hold Katie and Angela, your iron breasts," he said, rubbing his palms on my nipples in circles as he gently pressed each one into my chest.

We were seated on the bed. The mirror was behind one side so that I could study him as he moved. His movements were languid. Slow. Steady. Confident. He was nuzzling his head into my breasts. Running his tongue around a nipple. "Mustn't forget about Angela," he said as he focused on my other breast.

I ran my fingers through the hair that I adored. It was a black that reminded me of that stallion in the movie *Black Beauty*. When I held his face with my palms and looked into his dark brown eyes, I was under his spell.

"It's time to open the boutique," he said, as he unzipped my jeans and pulled down my pink bikini panties. He held them to his nose and sniffed them. "I love the smell of your *petite langouste*," he said, his eyes giving me that magnetic stare. "Let me take a look at the dimples on your *fesses*," he said as he turned me over and spread the cheeks of my buttocks. He held my ass firmly rotating his palms in a circular motion like he had held my breasts. Then he turned me over again to face him.

He moved his fingers down my thighs, which he squeezed in his firm grasp. His hands had magic to them and made me feel wanted. Loved. Captured . I had always done everything I could to prevent being caught. I often felt trapped in my marriage to Ron, but I never felt trapped with Claude, at least not in the beginning.

"It's time to open that boutique," he said, rubbing my rosebud, the door of the boutique, the handle that let out all that moisture and pleasure that had been waiting to be released. I became wet. Felt swollen. "Let me have a taste of your *langoustina*," Claude said as pushed me down on the bed and put his mouth between my legs. He ran his tongue around my lower lips.

I sighed.

He pushed my legs up to my breasts and nuzzled his face between them. He made a slight noise with his lips. The vibration quickly caused me to have an orgasm. Claude did this like no other man. I felt free . Floating over the Manhattan skyline.

Now he pushed his weapon deep into me in long, slow thrusts. I wanted him to stop. I didn't want to love him anymore than I already had. I was afraid of my love for him.

"*La boutique est ouverte*," he said, whispering into my ear as he ran his tongue around its edges. Then he laughed slightly. He knew he had control of me. I hated to relinquish control. Especially to men. "It is open for zee buziness," he said as he moved faster, still with that grin on his thick lips.

I was holding onto his taut biceps. Then his *rupettes*. He liked me to scratch them when the moment came close. His face was above mine. His gaze was like a laser beam that ran its power through my soul.

There was no music on the stereo. We were making love in silence. The only sound was the thrusting of his *zizi* deep into me. It sounded like galoshes stomping through the rain. The moment had come. We had come. We both let out screams and it was over.

The boutique closed for the night. *Ferme.*

Carole and Claude 1974

City of Lights

Early one morning in the winter of 1973, I flew to Paris and Claude fetched me at Orly Airport outside of Paris. He drove an old Renault that hadn't seen a car wash since the rainy season—or not, since Parisian weather year round was rain. French precipitation seemed to be Paris crying about its past. Constant storms made umbrellas almost as important at the franc.

From the back of Claude's Renault along with his photography equipment, briefcase, and stacks of *Le Monde*, tumbled, tail first, the second love of my life--Tutu, Claude's black teacup poodle.

"I've missed you, my Carolette," Claude said, putting his arms around me and kissing me. "Willkomen to Parigi, my neck of the woods, and this is *mon petit fils*, Monsieur Espresso."

We embraced and between us held Tutu who licked our chins and nibbled at my hair. Then we drove off to Grandmother Gilot's.

Grams's *crème*-colored carriage house had a rose garden in the backyard and bougainvillea by the front door. It was at *dix-neuf* rue Jacques Dulud in Neuilly. It had a garden that Tutu ran around in, Grams took walks in and Paloma gave cocktail parties in. A spiral staircase with a rosewood banister connected all three floors. In the living room the furniture remained covered in plastic throughout my seven-year relationship with Claude. (Years after, in a photo I would notice that the plastic was removed for Claude's wedding--to another woman.)

Tutu in front of Grams's carriage house

A tiny dining room, only big enough for a round table and four chairs, became the family headquarters. All activities, decisions, arguments, meals, litigation, etc. happened here. A portrait of Françoise Gilot painted by Picasso hung on one of its hunter-green walls.

Dr. Jonas Salk, Françoise Gilot, and Aurelia Simon

The kitchen, the biggest room on the first floor, competed with the dining room as the hub for family planning. It had heat, which made it popular. I have always been cold in Paris. Despite the damp climate, Parisians resist American heating facilities. Perhaps this is why they make such beautiful sweaters.

Most of the second floor belonged to Grams. Her bedroom was filled with sturdy, expensive mahogany antiques. Adjacent to Grams's, a miniscule guest room was used by Paloma when she was in Paris. It was also used by Aurelia, Claude's half-sister, when she visited Neuilly.

All in all the carriage house had the feeling of a metro stop at rush hour.

"*Voilà*," Claude said, opening the door to the third-floor bedroom. Antiques were artfully strewn about. As cluttered and random as the placement of objects seemed, they had an aesthetic look and feel. That is, the chaos was well-designed. On one wall was a landscape painted directly on the wall.

Tutu scampered onto the bedspread and barked.

"Who painted the cumulus clouds?" I asked.

"Paloma," Claude said, frowning. "I painted the barn and the cattle. Aurelia did the ducks and the pond. Françoise is threatening to draw a tropical rainforest on that wall. And Grams did this baby chicken."

While the paintings were charming, they added to the feeling of chaos and confusion.

"Where is Jonas's contribution?" I asked.

Claude laughed and wiggled his hands like Charlie Chaplin. "Jonas does not want to get involved. He contributes cerebrally to the Gilot/Salk union. The Gilot side provides the aesthetics. Thus the merger works. He claims to admire our visual talents." Claude feigned a cough.

I wondered if I could sleep in a bedroom that reminded me of the supply room when I taught children art.

"Let me show you the bathroom," Claude said, grabbing my hand.

We walked down the long corridor with its high ceilings and creaking floorboards. Tutu's tiny paws followed, clickety clack.

The toilet had no lid or handle. Instead a chain hung from the ceiling. "Who painted the toilet seat gold?" I asked.

"Paloma. For royalty, no doubt. Or a royal flush."

I didn't laugh. The bathroom was hideous.

"French humor doesn't translate," Claude said.

I nodded.

Tutu, not keen on the bathroom either, tugged at his master's trousers.

"My darling, I'm late for a meeting. Make yourself at home. Grams is out. You'll meet her tonight."

"Are you really leaving me alone?" I asked.

"Non, I'm leaving you with Monsieur Tutu." Claude patted his dog's tiny head.

"I've got to see my agent, but I'll be back at 5. We'll have dinner early."

"Are we going to eat here?"

"No, I'll take you to the Left Bank later. Brasserie Lipp. People look a little boring on the Champs-Élysée and in this neighborhood. Very bourgeois. You must sleep. With the time change and the excitement, you must be exhausted."

"I feel uncomfortable. Cold."

"I'll put this heater by the bed." Claude plugged in a small portable heating unit. "Now listen, my darling, you wanted to see Paris. *Voilá!* I warned you, it's different. French people always take you out. That's why there are the good restaurants."

Good, I thought. I wanted to get out of this cold carriage house, or whatever the fancy-pants French chose to call this latter-day monastery.

"Hardly ever are people invited into the home," Claude said, oblivious to my discomfort. "Unless you belong already in the household in one way or another. French people are funny that way."

My impression of French people was that they were cold and didn't like Americans.

"A home is where you hide. Where you should have privacy. A retreat. You should feel honored to be invited to Grams's.

Picasso's Ghost

Grams and Tutu

Not only do I want you here, but she does, too. She's very excited to meet you. Now rest, my Chérie."

Still wearing my wool pants, turtleneck, and socks, I crawled under the covers. Tutu, or Espresso, joined me. Claude kissed my forehead and I was asleep in no time. I dreamed of a greasy cheeseburger, yellow cabs, and the Statue of Liberty.

During our two-week sojourn, we visited the tiny town of Paulette, outside Aix, and took a quick trip to Cannes, as well as one to Chartres. Espresso followed us like a lamb everywhere we went.

Each day I enjoyed a French lesson with Grams, who after Claude and Tutu became the third love in my Parisian life. "She's a bit dyke-ish—like your mother," Claude would say. "That's why you like her."

Ignoring his insult to my mother and to Grams, I continued to admire Grams. She was my one friend in Paris and I cherished her companionship. Grams had short grey hair and wore sneakers and the same purple sweater five days in a row. She was a formidable miser. At the age of 70 she rode a motorbike, not slowed down one whit by a recent accident. In her youth hiking had been her passion. She never liked Picasso and was opposed to Françoise's love affair with him.

Grams's sense of humor was charming. When someone needed toilet paper on one floor, she delighted in throwing the roll down or up to the needy floor. Playing with Tutu was her favorite pastime. She would play with Espresso on her bed, swinging a two-liter Évian bottle over his head, saying in a singsong voice, "OH, Oooo, OH, ooo" as he would nipped at the bottle, trying to pull off the label.

Problem: Grams didn't speak English and my French was *caniche Francais*, which meant French for the dogs. To help us relate, every afternoon I visited Fauchon and chose a different selection of pastries that could be used as teaching aids to improve my vocabulary. My *gentillesse* gained me ten pounds.

"Carole, *c'est le sucre*," Grams said, pointing to sugar. "*Ça va?*" she said, asking if I understood.

And I would nod in agreement as I took a bite of *un gateau*.

Our conversations were never more enlightening than this, but I learned from Grams that words were not the only means of communication. That I could love someone without being able to make myself understood in words.

When we finally were able to relate, she told me the French were a nuisance, saying not to pay any attention to their petit bourgeois attitudes. Grandmère herself was of the *grand bourgeoisie*, I believed—but I'm not sure she would have agreed with my opinion.

Try as I could to understand the reclusive nature of the French, the chilly side of French culture remained an enigma to me. I slept with my socks on every night and my sneakers nearby. I told myself that I wasn't trying hard enough. Time and learning the language would help me to fit in. *Sans* doubt.

On my birthday January 8, 1973, Françoise had a surprise for me. It was as though she had picked up on my feelings of alienation. We were seated in the tiny dining room having coffee with my thirty-first birthday cake when Françoise handed me a paper envelope that could have come from a Five and Dime. Though she could match the grandest of Parisians in pretense at a party or for business, among friends Françoise was without guile. Inside the envelope was a piece of jewelry designed by Picasso with portrait of Claude carved into a rectangular medal about the size of two large postage stamps. Its asymmetrical form enhanced its beauty. The name CLAUDE, with the letter U looked more like a Roman V, was carved across the top of the medal. "Picasso created Claude's miniature portrait with dental tools," Françoise said, running her fingers over the tiny sculpture. "It was his first attempt at lost wax. I want you to have it."

I thought Claude would object, but he was pleased, holding me in his arms me as I studied the piece. At this time he owned only two small drawings by his father.

The pendant showed a portrait of Claude in profile at age five. Alfalfa-like stands of hair were carved loosely and unevenly, cascading down to the ear. The upper eyelid was visible, the nose was vague, and the chin and the mouth had been rubbed out. The neck was strongly indented. The expression in the eye was one of innocence. I wondered why there was no mouth. Was Picasso making a comment about Claude? Children? Was it happenstance?

The following night an angry Claude came into the kitchen carrying a copy of France's equivalent of the *National Enquirer*.

Françoise was preparing dinner.

"Look at this *merde*," Claude said shouting. "Paloma's done it again. It's that soft porno film she made, *The Immoral Tales*. The Polish director, supposedly an *artiste*, is going to show it at the Cannes Film Festival this spring."

"Don't let Grams see that," Françoise said, grabbing the magazine. "It's good Paloma is in Greece."

Later that night I read the piece below the screaming headline. "Paloma Picasso, star of *The Immoral Tales*, plays a vampire queen who amuses herself by bathing in the blood of freshly killed virgins making up her court. In the film a nude Paloma Picasso rubs sheep's blood over what most people consider their private parts, but keeps on her thick diamond necklace and crown." There was a photo of Paloma in full frontal nudity rubbing her breasts and pubic area with blood.

Françoise burned the magazine.

I hadn't met Paloma yet and now was secretly looking forward to it. She was the rebel in the family who frequented the homosexual disco, Le Club Sept. Françoise and Claude felt Paloma was exploiting the name Picasso with her jewelry designs, which embarrassed them. With Paloma's success in Greece with the esteemed jewelry designers Zolatos, Claude and Françoise had stopped belittling her. The respected art historian David Douglas Duncan referred to Paloma as inheriting her father's talents. Claude's competition with Paloma had surfaced. He obviously felt jealous, but tried to hide it by ridiculing her artistic talents.

Claude and Paloma

At times like this being a guest was downright awkward. I longed for New York. I wanted to go home. Claude's Paris hadn't been the festive, fun Paris I had known with Ron. No Régine's. No nightclubs. No four star restaurants. No fun discos like Castel. NO ENGLISH-SPEAKING TELEVISION! Once a week there was a movie in English. Sunday night. This was a big stay-at-home night for us expatriates

Claude led the life of a recluse. And now with the Paloma scandal he would be even more guarded. He never did photograph Dominique Sanda—which depressed him, not me.

I missed my work. The activity of modeling. Going to the Bahamas for a commercial. Shooting an ad for Chevrolet in San Francisco. My clients: Revlon, De Beers diamonds, Clairol, Fabergé. I missed the photographers and their silly pretentiousness. I missed the phone ringing. For me.

The next day we left from Paris. It felt good to return to 333 East 69th Street. Especially with our new family member—Tutu.

Now I could be my own woman.

Well, I would try.

Death and Marriage

On April 9, 1973, at midnight Claude and I were sleeping in each other's arms.

The phone rang. I answered it.

"This is the *New York Times*," a man's voice said. "Is Claude Picasso in?"

"It's for you, Chérie," I said, handing him the phone.

As Claude listened to the reporter, his face became contorted. "My father's dead!" He threw down the receiver and pounded the bed. "*Merde!Merde! Merde!*" he cried.

"I knew it would happen this way. Now my nightmares might end!"

When he could cry no more, Claude allowed me to hold him through a sleepless night.

All I could do was try to comfort him and let him know I cared.

On the first available flight the next morning, we flew to Marseilles to stay with his half-sister, Maya. (In 1977, four year after Picasso's death, her mother, Marie-ThérèseWalter, Picasso's long-term mistress after his first wife and before his mistress Dora Maar, would hang herself.) Blonde, robust, and mannish, according to Françoise Gilot's description in *Life with Picasso*, Maya had the beauty of a hearty German *fraulein* and the Teutonic sensibilities to match. She lived in three small rooms above a *tabac* in the port of Marseilles with her unassuming husband, who repaired boats.

After I was introduced to Maya, behind my back I heard her whisper, "Who is she and why is she here?"

When Paloma arrived, the talk began about what would happen to Picasso's estate, valued at several billion dollars. The abuse inflicted by Pablo upon his children was apparent when I heard them speak. Paloma spoke with a lisp. Her beauty had not yet been perfected. She had a prominent chin and wore red lipstick that contributed to her dramatic, mannish presence.

Picasso's genes were so dominant that he had sired women who looked masculine and resembled him. Short, quiet and observant, Paloma did not talk much. Until Picasso's death, Paloma's porno film, *The Immoral Tales*, had been the chief concern of the family. Now this family was focused on how to get to Picasso's wealth.

Maya resented Claude's authority and behind his back said he was ineffectual and could never be the head of the estate. Maya didn't trust Paloma and thought she was incompetent, saying this whenever Paloma was not in the room. Maya also thought Paolo, Claude's half-brother, was not bright enough in business affairs; therefore, he could not be the head of the estate. Paolo had refused to come to Marseilles.

So that I would not hear any conversations regarding the division of property or paintings, I was frequently asked by Maya to go to the *tabac*.

"Carole, get me a pack of Gauloises," Maya would command.

Around the kitchen table, covered in faded blue-checkered oilcloth, Claude, Paloma, and Maya sat listening to the radio. Suddenly one station announced, "During the night a huge caravan secretly transported the body of the greatest genius of our century, Pablo Picasso, from his villa in Mougins to his Château des Vauvenargues, a medieval castle not far from Aix-en-Provence."

"Why is he being moved?" Claude said, pounding his fist into the wall.

"I'll bet Jacqueline wants to ship his body to Spain," Maya said, shouting.

"That's not possible." Paloma said, crying.

"Over my d-dead body," Claude said. "He hated Spain. Bet she tries to do a deal with the government for a museum. Let's go to Vauvenargues."

Without hesitation Claude, Paloma, and Maya decided to drive to the Château des Vauvenargues in an attempt to bid farewell to their father. However, Jacqueline Roque, Picasso's widow, was now in charge of where he would be buried. Of Picasso's seven castles, the *Chateau* des Vauvenargues was the most austere.

The radio was our only means of knowing what Jacqueline might do. It was our only means of communicating with the dead. Paloma, Maya, Claude, and many of Picasso's friends blamed Jacqueline Roque for Picasso's banishing his children from his life as well as his hermitical existence in his later years.

While visiting Cannes this past winter, Claude and I had passed Jacqueline on the sidewalk. She nodded to me as she walked by, but then she quickly walked on. Like her portraits she was plump and quite plain with black hair combed tightly into a chignon. I thought she was beautiful. Carrying a large straw basket, she was mild-mannered and cordial to Claude, who was equally polite. They exchanged a *bonjour* as only the French can do, while beneath this façade of politesse ran decades of hatred because it was believed that she was the woman who had turned Picasso against his own children.

"I knocked her out unconscious once, supposedly j-joking," Claude told me. "My father thought it was very funny. But I meant it, you know. There was a wrestling match on TV and I said to my stepmother, 'Ha ha. You should have seen what this guy did to the other one.' And I, WHAAA! in the face. I didn't mean to, but I actually meant to, you know, and I flattened her out."

Perhaps Claude's violence towards Jacqueline had influenced her decision to keep Picasso from Claude.

Shortly before Picasso banished Claude, Claude had acted out in a variety of ways to get his father's attention. One way was to demand Picasso's limousine to drive Claude to rock concerts. Around the same time, Françoise was often too busy with her painting to be with her son.

Jacqueline, who had a daughter with a previous husband, was unable to have children with Pablo. According to the Gilot side of the family, this accounted for her seething contempt for Paloma, Françoise, and Claude.

And while Françoise was the daughter of wealthy bourgeois parents from the affluent Parisian suburb of Neuilly, Jacqueline Roque was the niece of a local potter from the town of Vallauris in the south of France, where she and Picasso lived.

Jacqueline Roque guarded the last years of Picasso's life from any interruptions to his creativity. Claude repeatedly would try to see his father, but was told at the gates of Picasso's villa that *"Monsieur* is not in." Meanwhile Claude would watch deliverymen allowed onto Picasso's property.

Upon the Great Master's death Jacqueline Roque stood guard over Picasso's corpse. Maya, Paloma, and Claude were not going to allow her to prevent their right to pay their last respects. Françoise Gilot knew going to Vauvenargues was futile and never even came to Marseilles. Françoise knew Jacqueline was in charge of the funeral as she had been in charge of the last years of his life. Françoise had bid farewell to Picasso when she wrote *Life with Picasso,* which Picasso tried unsuccessfully to ban—unlike his children. Picasso sued to try to stop the publication of Françoise's book, but when she won the suit, he sent her a note congratulating her on her triumph. Then in retaliation he trumped Françoise by driving a spike into her heart when he exiled Claude and Paloma from his life forevermore.

Nevertheless, the sparring between Picasso and Françoise continued long after their life together ended. Picasso liked a challenge and Françoise gave him that. She fought fiercely for her book and for her children to get to Picasso's fortune. But she could not fight Jacqueline who, it was rumored, instigated Picasso's exiling Claude and Paloma from his life.

While Françoise had won the battle over her book, she lost her children's right to see their father. Claude and Paloma had simply lost him, which made Claude and Paloma very angry with their mother. Furthermore Françoise had walked out on Picasso over his infidelity, while she was unfaithful to him with Jonas Salk—another strike against her, in her children's eyes. This unresolved anger toward Françoise came between Claude's and my love. Loving a woman was difficult for Claude, who felt betrayed by his mother and his father. (Marriage and relationships were not sustained easily for either Claude or Paloma. Claude would divorce his second wife after many years of marriage. And Paloma would divorce her first husband after many years of marriage, marrying her gynecologist.)

In 1973, Françoise would not fight Jacqueline for her right to go to Picasso's funeral. Jacqueline proved to be a tougher adversary than Picasso, whom Françoise could manipulate and beat in legal battles. At the time of Picasso's death Françoise had a new life with Jonas Salk. During this period their love flourished. Dr. Salk had replaced Pablo Picasso in Françoise's heart—or so it appeared.

Paulo, Picasso's legitimate son, whose mother had been Olga Koklava, Picasso's first wife, had remained on speaking terms with his father. In fact, he had been Picasso's chauffeur. Paulo loved cars almost as though they were his children. In Paris he had a large collection of Rolls Royces, Bentleys and an Hispano Suisse or two. Miserly like his father, he would take the metro instead of a cab to the garage.

A few months before Picasso's death, Paulo had driven Claude and me from Paris to Cannes in one of his Rollses. When we stopped at a petrol station on the *autoroute*, Paulo said to the attendant, "*Touche pas* my car, *s'ilvous plait*."

The attendant, chamois in hand, looked perplexed.

"*Mon vieux*, I have my own chamois. No one touches my car." Paulo said, adding, for our benefit, "You cannot trust these attendants. You see I wash my own windows. It is my pleasure to take care of this car. It is my prize. *Mon ami*."

"Don't you let them fill the tank?" I asked,

"*Mais non*! These i-di-ots! Gas spilled on paint and the car is finished! *Pardonnez-moi*." Paulo stepped out of his Rolls, opened its trunk, took out his chamois and a bottle of red wine. "*Tu veux du vin*, Claude?" he asked as he chugalugged the entire bottle.

"*Non, merci*," Claude said.

"Does he drink and drive?" I whispered to Claude.

"Guess so," Claude said.

"*Allons y*," Paulo said after he had thrown away the empty wine bottle, washed his windows, and filled the tank.

For the remainder of the journey I sat captive in his Rolls, a prisoner of his reckless disregard of his own well-being and that of others. He drove like a maniac. When we arrived in Cannes, we gave a sigh of relief.

Two years later, after being awarded by the courts over $500 million, his share of Picasso's estate, Paulo, who was the only legitimate heir besides Jacqueline Roque, would die of cirrhosis of the liver. His children, Marina and Bernard and his wife, Christine, would inherit his fortune. Despite Paulo's alcoholism, I found him to be gentle and thoughtful, except when he was drinking.

In 1986, in the medieval castle of Vauvenargues at the age of 60 Jacqueline Roque would shoot herself to death.

Paulo had refused to join us on our drive to Vauvenargues. He did not want a confrontation with Jacqueline, with whom he still communicated. Claude viewed Paulo's behavior as "playing both sides."

Not long after Picasso's death, Claude would say, "Paulo's calling me all the time for this, that, and the other. He's becoming more and more dependent on me, which is great, but of course a burden. Also I'm afraid to be authoritarian with him as of yet and demand things from him as he is still shaky. I told him I wasn't about to forget what happened when my father died. A little g-guilt works wonders with him."

At sunset two days after Picasso's death, Paloma, Maya, her husband, Claude and I squeezed into Maya's old Citroën for our journey. Maya's husband drove. I was told to be quiet and to listen to the radio though my French was inadequate for this task. The family again discussed the estate and its prospective worth as well as strategies of entry into the village of Vauvenargues to avoid the press.

We passed through the town of Paulette, which Claude and I had visited. While I watched the countryside painted by Cezanne, Matisse, Braque, Van Gogh, and Picasso, I felt as if a museum had come alive. Its voices were in the car. Its paintings, now moving landscapes, surrounded us and were sinister to see at night. Deep purple shadows created by the moon cast eerie light upon these rolling hills that reminded me of sleeping giants. I heard Picasso's children cry and whisper as I studied Cezanne's mountains. Van Gogh had cut off his ear in a mistral in this countryside. He painted this country as well. The Great Masters all had been here. Picasso's ghost wasn't the only ghost with us this night.

"There's the Mont Sainte-Victoire!" I said to Claude,

"I know, Chérie. We're talking about our father. Please. Excuse us if we seem to be excluding you," Claude said abruptly.

Paloma fought tears.

Maya planned the attack.

I thought about my days as an art teacher in Lower Merion, Pennsylvania, and how my students would have loved to have been here with us. I remembered the day I took them to Philadelphia's Art Museum and how excited they had been by Post-Impressionism, my favorite period of art history. Now it was as though we were driving inside a living painting on the way to a medieval castle for the funeral of the most celebrated artist of our century. I was ashamed of my feelings. Though they cried (all except Maya), I was having an adventure. One I'd never forget. Picasso wasn't my father.

I thought about the probability of my father's death in the near future. The scar tissue from the lobotomy was creating havoc in his brain. There would be a time for tears for my own father. Why weep along with Paloma and Claude? Instead I would try to help them as best I could. Their sorrow had paralyzed their ability to think rationally. Maya was defiant. Paloma wept. Claude was enraged.

We reached Vauvenargues at night. Yet it looked like day. Cameras, television crews, reporters, floodlights were everywhere. The Son et Lumière of Picasso's death. In the valley between the mountains surrounding us stood the Château de Vauvenargues. Like a giant coffin. Beneath the castle over the years a medieval moat had been transformed into a graveyard.

"Make a right up that dirt road," Claude said to Maya's husband.

"Go up the mountain away from the press." Claude bent down. "Watch it! Duck! Here come the cameras!"

Claude, Paloma, and Maya crouched in the backseat hiding their faces. Crowds forced Maya's husband to stop. A photographer pushed his face against the window, saw no photo opportunity, and turned away.

Maya peeked out of the car. "Keep going," she whispered. "Park behind that big cypress.. So we can see the castle."

"Chérie, watch for movement," Claude whispered. "A coffin. A corpse. A body being carried in or out."

We parked in a secluded spot under the foliage of a tall tree. "You can sit up now," I said. "It's safe. The press is below by the castle."

Maya's husband and I were told to be on guard for paparazzi, but the photographers had ignored us because of our battered Citroën. Who would believe that Picasso's heirs, soon to be worth billions, would arrive at his funeral by such humble means? Picasso's ghost, maybe.

The towering cypress and the twisting olive trees brought back those feelings of being in a moonlit museum. I wanted to wipe away Paloma's tears. To calm Maya's anger. To soothe Claude's rage. I could do nothing except study the huge wooden castle door as it would open and close and listen to a radio. We kept watching for coffins, for people carrying things in and out. They wanted to know where Picasso was going to be buried, but nothing happened.

I prayed for their suffering to end. Whether Jacqueline Roque liked it or not, Picasso's spirit was with us.

After an hour of our futile vigil, I made a suggestion. "Let's drive to Aix and buy flowers."

"Where would we put them?" Claude said.

"On one of those graves down there," I said, pointing to the vast graveyard.

"How would we know which grave is his?" Maya said.

"What's it matter?" I said.

"He likes gladioli," Paloma said.

"Write a letter," I said.

"What's the p-point?" Claude said.

"What do you mean, 'What's the point?' His spirit," I said. "Write to his spirit. Let the world know you were here. And care. Don't let Jacqueline gag you."

"*Allons y!*" Claude said as Maya's husband turned on the ignition. And under the moonlight we sped down the winding dirt road into town. Although it was late, one flower shop remained open.

"Let's not all go in," Claude said.

"I'll buy them," Maya's husband said, parking the car.

"Get peach gladioli," Paloma said.. "A dozen. Peach."

Maya's husband returned with a dozen peach gladioli. "What do we write on?"

"Look in the trunk," Maya said.

Maya's husband rummaged through the trunk and held up something from a laundry.

"How about this? My shirt's wrapped in cardboard."

"Great," Claude said with a smile. It was the first smile of the night.

"What do we write with?" Maya said.

Paloma pulled a green crayon from her purse. "Will this do?"

"Terrific! Now what do we say?" Claude paused. "How about, 'To our father whom we have loved and will love...forever...?'"

"*Au revoir...*" Paloma said.

"*À bientôt...*" Maya said.

Claude wrote the letter. Picasso's children signed it in silence. Maya's husband started the car and we drove back to the castle. It was about 10 PM when we pulled off the road and parked by the graveyard, some fifty feet below.

"Take off your shoes and socks," Claude said. Barefoot, we five descended to the graves. Some were open, with mounds of dirt piled by new tombstones.

"One of these must be for your father," I said. "If we run dirt through our fingers, we'll know which grave is the most recent. Soil freshly dug smells damp."

As absurd as it now seems, Picasso's children followed my advice. For over an hour we wandered aimlessly among the many open graves. The moon cast an eerie light over all while the castle remained a shadow looming in the distance. It was cold. Our feet were covered with dirt. I never left Claude's side.

Suddenly he stopped, embraced me, gazed into my eyes and said, "Will you be my wife?"

Though I was unprepared for the question, I knew the answer. "I would be honored to be your wife," I said beneath the starlight.

"I'll be the best husband you'll ever have, my Carolina, and the last."

We kissed and while Claude held me, I never felt so loved, wanted or safe in his arms as this night that Picasso died. Now perhaps Claude could live. . No longer tortured by his father's rejection.

Maya and her husband and Paloma, who had been carrying the letter, joined us. "Carole has agreed to be the next Madame Picasso," Claude said, and one by one they congratulated me.

Paloma placed the cardboard letter by the closest mound of soil. "I give up," she said. "Will this grave do?"

"It doesn't matter where you put it," I said.

"He'll get the message," Claude said as we knelt by an open grave and said the Lord's Prayer. Claude led us in "Our father…"

As we cried, I felt Picasso smiling upon us. Finally his spirit, now free, could be with his children . After we dried our eyes, we hurried back to the car and drove out of Vauvenargues, past the hordes of photographers still watching the castle.

"Stop the car," I said, shouting. "Tell the press to go down into the graveyard and to look for your message to your father."

Claude rolled down the window as I shouted at the paparazzi just that. A few looked at the battered Citroën in disbelief. They could not image a Picasso relative riding in a jalopy. Then we drove back through the land of Cezanne and onto Marseilles where we slept peacefully at last.

The next day I bought all the newspapers hoping to find a photo of the family's message to Picasso. But no photo. No word. And the world never knew about the beautiful gladioli Maya, Paloma and Claude bought for their father the night after his death. Picasso's children were too filled with guilt and shame for his rejection and their stepmother's to let the world know how they cried this night as they tried to bid their farewell.

Within a couple of days we drove to Cannes to meet Paulo, who joined the family for serious discussions about the estate. Then Claude and I returned to New York.

A few weeks later we read that Picasso had been buried in a crypt outside the entrance of the Château de Vauvenargues. While we had not found his grave, we had found his spirit.

Rags (but Rejected) to Riches

In the spring of 1974, the Bucks County Playhouse in New Hope, Pennsylvania, cast me in the play *Picnic* by William Inge. I was to play Madge, the role played by Kim Novak in the film version. Having just returned from the audition, I was eager to share the news with Claude, who was about to walk Tutu.

"Chérie, that's great," he said, squeezing my bottom. "But I don't like being separated."

"Come to Bucks County, Claude."

"Not so simple. I have affairs to attend to in New York."

"What affairs?" I said, assuming he was joking.

"That shoot for *Brides* magazine They want me to photograph you. Will you do it for me?" Tutu pulled at his leash.

Being photographed for *Brides* did not pay well and would not be especially prestigious. But I would do it to be photographed by Claude so that we could work together. "Of course I will, Claude, after I do the play. Please come and stay with me for two weeks?"

"A stage door Johnny? Not me. I'll visit." Claude tapped the top of my head and laughed sarcastically.

"My parents will lend you their car."

"That's nice of them, Cocotte, but I have to stay near the phones."

"They have phones in Pennsylvania," I said, hands on hips.

"Chérie, you don't get it. I wouldn't feel good about myself, sitting around while you're working."

"But you don't work in New York."

"Ah, that's unfair. You know I'm freelance and have to hustle for assignments. I shoot for *Vogue, Life,* and *Look* and write for the *Saturday Review* sometimes. One day you're going to regret your ball breaking. I'm warning you."

"You pick your hours. You could choose to be with me."

"Carolina, someone's got to mind the store, as you say. And it's got to be me."

Claude waved his forefinger mockingly at me as Tutu yanked on his leash. "Besides we have Monsieur Tutu to think of. He's no stage door Lassie either."

I frowned. Tutu barked.

Claude opened the door. Tutu ran out.

Claude, Tutu and Me

While I performed in Bucks County, Claude called me every day. One call was special.

"I won! TOTALLY! Françoise phoned from court. The French government abolished the Napoleonic Code because of Françoise's lawsuit. Françoise beat Napoleon. And my father. Now the government will legally have to give us my father's fortune," Claude said in a high-pitched voice.

"Is that why you stayed in New York?"

"I didn't want to tell you in case we lost. I knew Françoise was at court. You don't have to worry anymore! How's it feel?"

"I can't believe it. How do you feel?"

"I-I don't know." Claude paused. "I'm free now. I'm going out of my head because I can't express to anyone how I feel. My darling, I can't talk. I need you."

"Come to Bucks County?"

"I'll be down tonight. Françoise said I was on the front page of every French paper. I don't know what to do. It's been such a long time coming. I feel wasted, yet like I can do anything and no matter what it is, it will be OK."

"It's more than OK. It's what you deserve."

"The papers say at a minimum I should have six million. What's that mean?"

"I don't know what one million means."

"It'll be much more when I take over the family. And I will."

"Don't forget what Francis Coppola said at Marie Brenner's party."

"What's that?"

"Ah, you see, you forgot already."

"Save the guilt, Chérie."

"Coppola said you should give your money away. Too much money's a bad thing."

"Has he done that?"

"Actually he has. He's been bankrupt several times because he's invested his own money in his projects."

"Don't worry. I'll buy your wedding dress. If that's what you're getting at." Claude laughed.

"Your mother said she wants to, so you're too late. Are we going to Paris?"

"Next week. When you finish the play. Jonas tried to call you, but your line was 'busy, busy', so stay off the blasted phone, Chickadee, please. Life's going by and all you do is yackity yak."

"I'm lonely."

"Read a book."

"I'm too lonely to concentrate."

"If you'd turn off the rock n roll, maybe you'd know what's on the page."

"Music makes me happy."

"Books make you intelligent AND happy."

"I don't like that remark, Claude."

"Sorry, didn't mean it like it sounds. Books would make you more intelligent and happier." Claude paused. "Oh, Françoise said to bring toilet paper."

"What?"

"We're covering Grams's house in toilet paper. France only has stacks of sheets for toilet paper. We are in the Middle Ages in that department. Françoise wants Charmin for that international soft touch."

"Get Scott. One thousand sheets to a roll. It's cheaper."

"Carolina, we don't have to save on anything ANYMORE," Claude said, shouting. "Let alone toilet paper."

"How's it feel to be rich?"

"Wasted. Wonderful. Words can't describe it. I'll show you tonight, my *langouste*.

"Oops, Tutu peed on the bed. He misses you, too. *Ciao, mon amour*."

The following week Claude and I flew to Paris to celebrate with the family. Françoise,

Grams, Aurelia, Jonas, Paloma, and I covered Grams's carriage house in toilet paper. The banisters, the doors, the chandeliers, all three floors appeared to be covered in pastel streamers. Paloma even brought a few rolls from Greece.

The next day Françoise and Paloma invited me to the salon of Karl Lagerfeld, from whom Françoise ordered my wedding dress. It was salmon, midcalf length; it fell just below my knees and had tiny pearls trimming its crepe de chine bodice. A horsehair picture hat and dyed-to-match shoes from Maud Frizon completed my ensemble. When I tried on the entire outfit, I looked as if I'd walked out of a painting by Renoir—rather than one by Picasso.

While I was trying on the dress, Paloma wanted to come into the dressing room with me. "Let me help you get into the dreth," she said with a lisp. As I stood there in my underwear, I felt Paloma's eyes studying my body as though she were a man taking in every detail. Quickly I dressed and vowed never to be nearly naked in front of Paloma again.

When we returned from Karl Lagerfeld's, Françoise surprised me with yet another Picasso, a sculpture. "This is your engagement present," she said.

"Oh, my," I said, kissing her on her cheeks. "You are too kind." About the size of a fist, it resembled a Mexican sun. An uneven oblong shape, it rose at the center as though it were a tiny volcano with a smiling face. The nose, again reminiscent of genitalia, was its pinnacle. The mouth, a semicircle, was awkwardly drawn, off-center. The eyes were round with dots for pupils. One eyebrow curved up while one curved down. At the base of the raised volcano-like face, lines were carved irregularly, giving the impression of bursts of sunlight. Seven round protrusions surrounded its base.

In all, it had a lopsided goofy feeling to it, the work of a child at play.

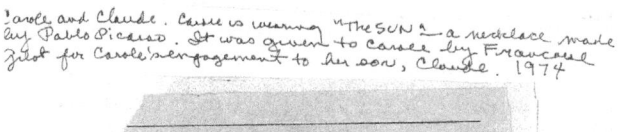

Carole and Claude. Carole is wearing "THE SUN"—a necklace made by Pablo Picasso. It was given to Carole by Françoise Gilot for Carole's engagement to her son, Claude. 1974

Claude and I wearing the Picasso piece as a necklace.

When I looked at my petite Picassos, I was fascinated with Picasso's sexual images. I couldn't help wondering what it would have been like to have had sex with him. Françoise did not address this in her book, *Life with Picasso*, but I wondered if he made love like Claude. Claude's orgasm was loud and volcanic. I wondered whether the sun piece was reminiscent of how Picasso felt during an orgasm, and why he made the nose into the shape of a penis.

Once back at Grams's carriage house, Paloma held court in her miniscule bedroom while wearing high-heeled shoes, jewelry, a hat, and nude pantyhose, but no skirt. As she talked to Claude about my wedding dress, she was sprawled on her bed with her legs spread and her pubic hair visible through the nylon pantyhose because she was not wearing panties.

I remembered that Claude told me that because he looked so much like his father, Paloma confused him with Picasso, like Françoise did. Prior to Claude's becoming the head of the estate Paloma would make her feelings known by acting as though Claude were the head of the family. She would flatter his ego and make him feel empowered, then she would act helpless. After Claude actually became the administrator of the estate she was especially helpless when it involved something she did not want to do, like help Claude settle the estate. This difficult and tedious task she delegated solely to Claude while she pursued her jewelry designs and a jet set life style.

Dr. Jonas Salk enjoyed all the superficial glamour that was Paloma's preoccupation. Grandmère called it *la vie mondaine*. While Jonas seemed attracted to Paloma's beauty and the exciting life she led , Paloma's concentration was on provoking her mother. Paloma's unresolved anger towards Françoise for writing *Life with Picasso*, for leaving her father, and for herself being unfaithful in turn with Jonas were the driving forces for Paloma's cruelty to her mother.

When Françoise first left Picasso she married Luc Simon, who was an actor who portrayed Lancelot in Bresson's *Lancelot du Lac*. Shortly after Françoise married Luc, she gave birth to Aurelia. Françoise told Claude that Luc Simon was a homosexual. She must have meant bisexual since he was the father of Aurelia. But Claude had told me the term homosexual was Françoise's way of implying that Luc was handicapped in the masculinity department—which Claude was not.

Claude loved Françoise's attention and affection. Above all he liked the idea that because he looked like Picasso, he could almost be Picasso, who was the one Françoise truly loved.

Often Claude and I lunched at the Petit St. Benoit, a restaurant on the Left Bank frequented by students. My favorite dish was *hachis parmentier*. Waitresses took your order on the paper tablecloth, which was replaced for each seating. There were tables outside on the street and in the summer clowns, magicians, musicians, and actors performed during dinner, afterward passing a hat.

One summer Aurelia, who was studying mime and ballet, performed for the customers. With Aurelia's father, Luc Simon, Paloma would come to this restaurant arm and arm. The next evening Aurelia with her father, Luc Simon, would come arm in arm.

I do think Luc Simon and Paloma knew each other well. When Luc wasn't coming on to Paloma, Luc was flirting with his own daughter, Aurelia. He played one against the other.

Every day Claude was busy with the estate. I wandered around Paris with Tutu.

Claude was gaining confidence and becoming brusque, which I realized was due to the pressure he was under. He was preparing to inventory his father's art.

Time was needed to unravel the estate; therefore, I offered Claude my life savings to tide us over. He had wanted a penthouse in New York and chose a two-bedroom apartment on the 31st floor of the Sovereign on Sutton Place. With a rosewood and marble lobby that extended from First Avenue almost to York Avenue and doormen wearing tails, caps and white gloves, it seemed our relationship was going corporate. In our elevator I would encounter Calvin Klein; Leo Jaffe, chairman of the board of Columbia Pictures; and film producer Alberto Grimaldi.

In my previous apartment our neighbors had been artists: KarelAppel, Isamu Noguchi, and Richard Lindner. Mark Rothko lived a block away. Claude's taste surprised me. When we'd met, he was definitely bohemian. His photojournalism concerned the working class. I was even more surprised when I read that Picasso *père* had said, "What I want is to be able to live like a poor man with plenty of money." On our first date Claude had told me how excited he was to be photographing a low-income housing project and interviewing people who lived there. One of his best friends had been Michel Laurent, a photojournalist who had been killed on assignment during the last days of the Vietnam War. Michel Laurent had been to my apartment. I'd cooked dinner for him. He would have worn khakis to a black-tie event at the White House. Claude had this spirit when we had met.

Still I didn't worry much about the change coming over Claude; I loved beautiful surroundings, too, and was far from your local communist myself.

Claude standing in front of my Chryssa sculpture

In Paris, Claude leased another apartment at 260 Boulevard St. Germain. It had eleven rooms, totaling 200 square meters. This enormous space for our teacup poodle, Tutu, and the two of us.

For our Parisian apartment we ordered a navy blue custom Dutch kitchen. For our car, Claude began looking at Bentleys.

I returned to New York without Claude in order to tend to our affairs.

In his first letter he wrote, "So many thoughts to say, to tell you with my fingers, my eyes, and whatever hair I have left. My body misses you. My tongue craves for the taste of your *langouste*—your tiny snore next to me at night, the warmth of your body each of your iron breasts in each of my hands, your round beautiful big cul against my stomach, grabbing you by the dimples above your *fesses*. I want to kiss you right now...,sticking my nose in your mane.... bury my face between your breasts. *Je t'aime*."

During one phone call he was particularly excited, which caused him to stutter. "Today Paulo asked me to b-be in a photo with him to show that we're now good friends as well as brothers. Isn't that terrific? Tomorrow w-we're going to an opening of Juan Gris and showing off together."

"That's great, Claude. Is he still drinking?" I asked. When, in fact, I was still drinking myself.

"Yep. What can I do?"

"What's happening with the car situation?"

"The Bentley dealer had a convertible with a special body and four doors. Scarce. Good price. You'll die when you see it. There's also an older type, square and small, but without power steering. You couldn't drive it."

"How's the kitchen?"

"I got a n-new estimate from the Dutch kitchen place and a new floor plan. I have to put money down Friday or it'll be 18% more."

"Are the painters O.K.?"

"I'll call them tonight. Paloma wants me to go to St .Laurent's fashion show with her tomorrow."

"Stay away from the models, Cherie," I said.

"What m-models?' Claude said, laughing. "Someone's at the door. I want your voice cooing against my shoulder. *À bientôt, mon amour*."

Was Paloma trying to fix Claude up with models? I wondered.

Stepford Wife

While Claude was achieving power and recognition in the art world, which previously had ridiculed him, I was beginning to struggle for my place in his life. Modeling had lost its appeal; however, acting still had an allure. How would I fit into his new life?

That winter, when Claude called me from Paris, I announced, "Claude, I have good news. I've been cast as a *Stepford Wife* in the film."

"You know I don't want you to act," he said, sounding miffed.

"I enjoy acting."

"Being my wife is not enough for you?"

"Don't look at it that way. I just can't do dishes for the rest of my life. That's not me."

"You'd hardly be doing dishes, Carolina. We will have a maid."

"Well, I can't go to charity luncheons for the rest of my life either."

"I didn't even know you went on the audition."

"Well, I wanted to surprise you," I said. Without telling Claude, I had met the director, Bryan Forbes. I had known Claude didn't want me to act.

"Did you read the script?"

"No, I just met with the director and he cast me based on my success with my TV commercials. They want perfect-looking female specimen types and that was me, I guess."

"When do you film?"

"In the spring. Only for a few weeks. In Westport, Connecticut."

"You are truly independent. Sometimes you remind me of Françoise."

Uh oh, I thought, and moments later we hung up.

I wanted a career of my own. I loved the theatre and the people in it and knew for my self-worth I needed to work at something that gave me pleasure.

Eventually Claude said he understood my decision to do the film and offered to plan our wedding from Paris. We were to be married at Maggie and Jerry Minskoff's home in East Hampton. Claude's godparents were close friends of the Minskoffs, who owned a New York theatre.

During the filming, I stayed in a hotel in Westport. After a few days of shooting, Claude called.

"How's my *Stepford Wife*?" Claude sounded in a good mood.

"I hate my costumes," I said. "If Paula Prentiss doesn't like her wardrobe, she cuts it up."

"You're not Paula Prentiss, Chickadee."

"Bette Davis visited the set. She let me take her photo. Everyone thinks she's sick because she wore a wig."

"Chemotherapy?"

"Maybe."

"How's Bryan Forbes's direction?" asked Claude, who still dreamed of being a director.

"Good. Caught me not listening to Katherine Ross in a scene. Made us do several takes."

"Glad someone else told you that you don't listen."

"What?"

Claude laughed. "You heard me. So where shall we go for our honeymoon? Morocco? Marrakech is hot. Not unbelievable, but hot. Air-conditioned. Swimming pools."

"Never been. Always wanted to see it. How about Tunisia or Bali?"

"Too far. Anything you like, my love, except Venice, France, and Spain. For obvious reasons...etc. etc."

"Can't wait for this film to be over. Too much tension. Paula Prentiss had a few drinks before my big scene between her and Katherine Ross. So Bryan Forbes yelled at her before he said, 'Action!' I had to keep the scene together."

"Your usual role, Chérie."

"Then Paula apologized to Bryan for flubbing her lines. He said, 'Don't apologize to me. Apologize to Carole.' Well, Katherine Ross was terrified. I was stuck in the middle of them at my kitchen table trying to keep harmony."

"Bet the scene's good because Paula did that. Made you forget yourself."

"Not bad."

"Probably funny."

"How'd you know?" I asked.

"Under pressure you're funny." Claude said.

Katherine Ross and Paula Prentiss and I while filming Stepford Wives

"Not laughing about the wedding. I'm nervous."

"Don't be. Françoise and I picked out a surprise for you. A piece of jewelry with emeralds and pearls."

"I've never owned precious stones. Let alone had them given to me." (This jewelry would never materialize.)

"Hurry up and finish playing that robotized wife and be my real one."

"I will, darling. Ten more days."

"I think if we get married on the 14th of July you might as well stay over there since I'll be spending day in and day out in cahoots with the lawyers for the estate. I'll have to apply for the marriage license. Can we plan for your freedom about the 30th of June?"

"I certainly hope so. How about the wedding cake?"

"CM plus CP forever or some such joke on it. I want Lenôtre to make it for some publicity number. But NO photos."

"Wish you were here. Westport isn't the same without you."

"We'll be together soon, Ma Chérie. *Guarder* that boutique."

"The boutique is out of business this side of the Atlantic, my love."

"That's good. Keep it closed. I miss your turquoise eyes."

"*Je t'aime*. Give a 'woof' to Tutu."

When the film was a few days from completion, I received a phone call from Claude, whose attitude seemed to have changed.

"*Allo*, Chérie. I just got your letter. You sound good, but I'm not so sure about the wedding dates. Now they conflict with my work with the l-lawyers," Claude said. His voice was strained.

"I thought you had made all the arrangements," I said, irritated.

"I'm under terrible pressure and think we should move the date to August or September."

"I was planning to be your wife in seven very long weeks. Who will tell the Minskoffs?"

"I will, Carolina. Look, Maya's the problem. Telling me Paulo doesn't agree with m-me when I just talked to him the minute before. I'm sure she's cutting a deal with Jacqueline. Maya's a troublemaker."

"Have you confronted Paulo?"

"It's delicate. He and Jacqueline have most of the estate. I only have 1/8th. I have to watch my words."

"You said you'd get at least six million. Six million is six million, Claude. Be grateful."

"I am, but still I'm doing the work. Paulo's calling me all the time and becoming dependent on me. It's a burden. Jacqueline's got all her lackeys calling up Paulo to ask if we've cut a deal."

"Have you?"

"Of course not. Paulo was smart enough not to tell anyone anything. This way they can think we have or have not. Information in legal matters transfers to money."

"Claude, I'd planned on the wedding in July. What'll I tell my parents?"

"We'll have to put it on hold. Until I come up from under this pressure. I'm very nervous. Trembling again."

"You ought to see a doctor about that. Can't Jonas give you medication?"

"It's just that I'm alone here. Paloma's in Spain. Françoise, Jonas, and Grams are in Venice. And you're in Connecticut. How's the shoot?"

"It's over soon, thank God. Can you believe Katherine Ross is marrying a grip. You know, he fixes things on the movie set. He's like a gofer. Well, he wouldn't even carry my bags from the train when I got here. What kind of husband will he make?"

"A grip!" Claude laughed.

"He's sexy and handsome and all that, but when he wouldn't carry my bags, which was his job by the way, I got suspicious."

"Carolina, come to Paris when you're done and we'll deal with the wedding together. Grams said we could get married in her garden."

"You mean you're not coming to New York at all?"

"No time. You know Berggruen, the art dealer. Well, he's teaching me fakes and compiling lists of the existing prints in my father's estate. I found over 25,000 prints when the previous inventory listed only 6,000."

"I remember when Berggruen used to patronize you, Claude."

"So he doesn't anymore. Look, it doesn't do any good to hold on to resentment. I need these guys and they need me. It's even-steven now. Don't remind me of the negativity of the past. I have a new life. And you do, too. Berggruen can help us."

"I hear you."

"These dealers are teaching me. The other day I made a half a million."

"How in the world did you do that?"

"I found out how I could convert the inventory into cash by taking a small loss. A small percent to the Bank of France. It's completely legal. Nobody thought of it. I asked an officer at the bank who said he'd do it right away. I cut lawyers fees in half by convincing the bank of the enormity of the amounts they could absorb without losing everything to the IRS and that lovely-dovey prick Giscard. And for all this, I'm only getting 1/8th. For all my good efforts."

"Don't be greedy. Six million is hardly a small percentage. Remember Francis Coppola."

"Save the guilt trip for your mother. I won't put up with nagging."

"I'm sorry," I said, not liking the authoritarian tone, which had become a part of the new Claude. "You should have been a lawyer."

"One lawyer in the family is enough. And that's Françoise. She's a barracuda in legal affairs."

"You're just a shark. I can see."

"For us. Don't forget. Meanwhile Paloma gave me her skin disease. The doctor gave me a treatment and the side effect is it might help my loss of hair."

"The more hair you lose, the more you look like your father."

"Don't you start. I have enough with Paloma and Françoise confusing me with him."

I remembered Françoise playing into this confusion and justifying Claude's love for her. Her justification was that because of his father's rejection, in certain psychological theories, Claude should be a homosexual. She felt it was better for Claude to love her and remain a heterosexual. The family talked about how she promoted this.

"When do you want me in Paris?" I asked.

"As soon as you can get here. And we'll reschedule our connubial bliss."

"You're not getting cold Spanish feet, are you?"

"My *langoustina*, I love you more than ever, but if you ever had to deal with lawyers, you'll know what I'm going through. Read Kafka's *The Trial*. The estate is truly a Kafkaesque nightmare. I need 100% of your support to make it to the other side."

"What's that?"

"Cash. Right now we have lots of paintings, sculpture, property, but we can't flood the market. Prices would drop. We need to learn to convert the estate into cash. Without damaging the value of my father's art. Meanwhile, I'm broke."

"I'm taking care of you, Claude. Not to worry. We have my $50,000. And our love and a big phone bill. But I have to ask you something?"

"What's that, Chérie?"

"I want a baby."

"Good Lordie. Again you ask me. Can't you wait until our honeymoon.?"

"I'll wait. You're worth it."

"Tutu sends you a big lick. *Et moi aussi, ma biche.*"

The real pain Claude caused me is that I wanted a child and he didn't. And it still hurts me deeply. I had never wanted to burden him before he was ready, but I couldn't help asking him often whether he wanted one. When his father died, I thought we could start planning, but he wanted to wait for the estate to be settled. This was going to be a monumental task, and I thought "easy does it" in the beginning. Claude had to adjust to the loss of his father. When he talked about Picasso, Claude sounded so lost.

"I lived very little with him," Claude would say. "I lived with him until I was like five, six, then visited on holidays. Like puppy dogs coming in and out of the house. And uh, then all of a sudden BOOM, no more, nothin'. You know at the age of fifteen or sixteen for no reason except that maybe my mo...my mother wrote this book and that might have infuriated him or we were just in the way and his wife didn't like us or whatever. We reminded him of the past."

It seemed to be that emotions from that time were surfacing when we were about to be married, thus his delay about setting a wedding date. (Eventually, when I left Claude, I told him that he was doing to me what his father had done to his mother and to him—eliminate the past.)

The family blamed Jacqueline Roque for closing the doors, not Picasso. That way the pain was lessened. I believed Picasso was responsible for the decision, a decision he made in part because he wanted his children to seek their own identity. There had been too much *"fils du papa"* behavior. Too much trying to imitate Picasso in his dress, manner, art, temper, love life. Day by day Picasso's children were allowing themselves to be swallowed up by his commanding persona.

"I told my father the truth, you know," Claude said. "I paid for it. I got the paintings through my head. My father asked me, 'What do you think of this?' I said, 'It ain't too cool. What the fuck? You gonna work on it again?' So the painting went right through my head."

"Next time I saw my father, he said, 'Come in here.' I said, 'That's really cool, y'know,' and he gave the painting to me. But the point of the story is it didn't do any good either way. You can't win. Because I never saw him again. I was nice, so I was discarded."

"By the age of fifteen, you know, I was going out to nightclubs in Paris and had girlfriends and when I was at my father's, all of a sudden this whole thing had to stop. I would say I wanted to go to a rock concert or some idiotic stupidity, little simple things that even children do in America (Claude would snap his fingers) like that! You know, right?'

"But it was, 'No! You have to keep the chauffeur all night.' 'No, no all the way.' And there was like no reason for it, you know."

"So we said 'Fuck it.' It was hassles, hassles, with the stepmother. Things like that."

Claude had a problem with humility, but he also was insecure and trying to overcompensate. He had tried to tell Pablo Picasso how to paint.

Picasso hadn't liked what was happening to Claude, nor had he liked being distracted by Claude's constant need for attention. The aggravation Claude caused was keeping his father from his work. Picasso was being drained of his talent, and he was not helping his children grow. In fact now his power and fame had become a hindrance to their growth. Picasso never wanted his children to have his name, but he did not stop Françoise when she made the necessary legal arrangements for them to be Picassos instead of Gilots.

Picasso was known to have said repeatedly that his name would bring no good to anyone other than himself.

Paloma Picasso, with her successful jewelry line at Tiffany's, proved her father wrong.

I wonder if her success was driven by revenge and her need to prove her worth to her father.

But it was Claude who suffered most from a lack of attention from both parents. He had fits of trembling along with stutter. Claude liked to talk about his father, but he also enjoyed talking about his mother.

According to my diary, he said, "Françoise was a little flippant and not even to this day very well-connected in her head. But she had liberal ideas. So children are free. They do as they want, you know. They have to learn to take responsibility. We had to find ourselves, you know. That was the idea."

"When we went to my father's house the simplest thing became a problem, I mean things that we were used to living with my mother. We would go riding horses, there was no problem. At my father's place it became a program. We had to ask the stepmother and she would say, 'go ask your father.'"

My father would say, 'Don't fuck with me. Ask your stepmother.' Then we'd say, 'But we need two dollars to do this'...."

"'Ah! Two dollars. What the fuck?' he would say. 'Whaddayou think? You're the son of Rockefeller?' So I'd say 'Huh?' Nothing made sense. There was always this kind of, 'Let's get rid of the situation. Go play. We have something else to do here,' you know."

In Françoise's book *Life with Picasso*, she wrote: "It must have been lonely for Claude and Paloma much of the time; they almost never saw their father and their mother barricaded herself behind her studio door whenever she could see a spare hour or two."

Françoise proudly talks of a typical day when she was busy painting and there was a knock at the door. She did not open it, but asked, "Who's there?"

The voice said, "Mama, I love you."

Françoise said, "I love you, too, my darling."

The voice said, "Mama, I like your painting."

Francois said, "Thank you, darling. You're an angel."

The voice said, "Mama, what you do is very nice. It's got fantasy in it, but it's not fantastic."

Françoise stayed her hand, but said nothing. She hesitated.

The voice spoke up louder now. "It's better than Papa's."

Françoise went to the door and let Claude in.

While Françoise was liberal in her care of her children, she was not liberal when it came to Claude's attempt to grow up on his own and to find an identity. She smothered him. Françoise would not allow Claude to do things on his own. She had her elegant, influential friends and was always scheming how to get Claude and Paloma prestigious jobs.

When Claude applied to the American Film Institute, he prepared a film, an essay, and all that. Mrs. Gregory Peck, who was French, was a friend of Françoise and Jonas and was going to make all the necessary *entrées* for Claude.

When we entered the forbidding building that housed the Institute, Françoise asked where Claude should go for the interview. The gentleman at the entrance indicated the proper direction, and Claude ascended the staircase with Françoise and me shortly behind him.

He turned around. There were words. He pleaded for her to let him do it alone, but she would not listen. He looked like a lost puppy dog. It was sad. No love from his father, and an overprotective mother. No wonder Claude had trouble finding his identity.

No wonder I have had trouble finding mine.

My father was not really there for me and I had an overprotective mother.

Claude and I had much in common—a search for identity. I was dependent on Claude and seeking my identity through him, and he was doing the same through me—until the death of his father.

Picasso's Ghost

Bohemian to Bourgeois

When I joined Claude in Paris after filming *Stepford Wives*, he had changed.

Wearing a three-piece suit and a tie, he met me at Orly with Tutu. "Chérie, good to see you," he said, grabbing my bag. Tutu tugged at my skirt. Claude kissed me briefly on my lips.

Pulling away from his embrace, I said "You've cut your hair, Claude. Why?"

"Oh, you can't be with lawyers all day and look like a hippie. They won't respect you or listen to you."

"I thought they work for you." I said, taking in his monogrammed shirt. "Is that the Brooks Brothers shirt I got you?"

"No, Chérie, this is Christian Dior. Sorry, but I don't have time to be with you for lunch. I have a meeting with an art dealer, but I'll take you to the apartment and maybe you can get some sleep. With the time change and all th-that."

Claude dropped me at our apartment and quickly left. What kind of reception was this? Tutu kissed my cheeks, and then we wandered around our eleven rooms now painted dark primary colors. Was Claude's behavior an indication of a new relationship for us?

As it turned out, it was. Claude was continually with the lawyers for the estate. I felt doors closing in on me. The possibility of my becoming a rich wife of someone who had a famous father made me feel like a hanger-on, excess baggage, a ghost whom everyone looked through on the way to finding the real Picasso—or better yet, one of his paintings. I would give these die-hard fans of Picasso no hope of a glimpse of history or gossip about the great genius, only a void. For those treasure-seekers I offered nada, nothing, ZIP! Like Mary's little lamb, the parody version, the vamp that Mary took to Pittsburgh. That was yours truly. The black sheep. Paris was Pittsburgh to my soul, showering down comparisons to Claude, Paloma, Maya, Françoise—"blah, blah, blah" to quote Claude. I didn't want to be compared to anybody, anything. I wanted to be free. To be. Becoming Madame Picasso was threatening my identity. And I was allowing it to...That was the clincher.

On the other hand, Claude was forging an identity out of his new wealth and the respect he now commanded (Oh, how many times I had heard that the art world belittled him.) Now he was caretaker of his father, his father's paintings, houses, gold, castles, investments, cash, drawings, jewelry, writings, sculptures. Everything Picasso owned was being cared for...inventoried...and would eventually be appraised by Claude. Caring for Picasso began to consume Claude's love.

I had placed myself in competition with Picasso's ghost. There was no way I was going to win that race, battle, or lawsuit. If only I had stepped back for a few years to allow Claude and myself to adjust!

Carole & Claude arguing at the Museum of Modern Art 1972

Claude and I arguing at the M.O.M.A.

I began to imagine that Claude was doing to me what his father had done to him. By wanting a career I had reminded Claude of his mother. Despite his adoration of Françoise, he had unresolved resentment toward her. She had had boyfriends in Paris while married to Jonas, had written "that book" and had given Claude the impression that her work was more important than he was. I, too, like my own father, was compulsive about work. Claude forbade me to pursue acting. In Paris I had few friends and had difficulty making new ones. My French was inadequate though I'd studied it and continued to study it. An American's French is rarely good enough for Parisians.

Claude was gone all day. Each night he refused to share his work—that is, estate matters—with me. I felt isolated, again like an apparition, and began to feel inadequate and unwanted. In the way.

I began to drink heavily. Blackouts began. I was forgetting what I had done the night before. What I had said. There was Valium every night. With wine.

My life was repeating itself. Heartburn with heartache. I was reliving the feelings I had when Ron and I separated. While I had not had blackouts when I was with Ron, I had taken Valium with wine. When Claude and I had fallen in love, my drinking had decreased. Now it was an aperitif, a bottle and a half of wine during dinner, and a cognac. After all, this was how the chic French drank, and I wanted so much to be accepted by them. But oh, how I hated to admit it.

By November 1974, we were still not married. The money from the estate had not been released. My wedding dress was one year old. Dusty. We were still living off of my savings. Yet each time I bought myself something, Claude demanded that he had the right to approve of the purchase. Which was paid for with my money. I gave him power and felt myself an appendage of his wants, needs, desires—while I was allowing my needs to be subjugated to his.

I gained ten pounds.

Each time I brought up the date of the wedding, Claude began to rage. Was he stalling? I wondered. I realized that when the estate's money came, I would be able to buy anything. Suddenly material things all looked the same. Boring. I wanted nothing. Shopping became a dull ritual motivated by loneliness. I wanted to work, but didn't know what to do. Whatever I chose to do would have to meet with Claude's approval; therefore, I did nothing. There were rules to being a Picasso. The 24-karat Golden Rule was, "You can't do anything that could tarnish the name."

Even Picasso's own daughter had to face this form of imprisonment. Could defiance of the sanctity of the name "Picasso" be the reason she appeared in full frontal nudity in the film *The Immoral Tales*?

The French would not sell her Tiffany jewelry because they did not approve of Tiffany's and Paloma Picasso's use of her father's name for commercial purposes.

My becoming the wife of a famous multimillionaire had the price tag of my freedom. Marrying Claude would have meant being his appendage instead of his partner. His off-camera *Stepford Wife*. In time Claude might have become more secure in his new role, and I might have found a life of my own among the Parisians, but circumstances were such that we would not be given this opportunity.

That November, while Claude and I were staying at the Hotel Majestic in Cannes, he was inventorying his father's villa, Notre-Dame-de-Vie, in Mougins. Claude had to oversee the documentation the government was making of Picasso's art. I was not allowed inside the villa. November is not a pleasant month in the south of France for a sun worshiper such as me. Claude would get up early and come home late, telling me very little of what he was doing with the estate. Again I felt left out. The excitement of seeing all of the things from the past was giving him more and more confidence, happiness, and a feeling of closeness to his father. But he was not sharing these feelings with me. I felt us drifting apart. Fortunately I had Tutu.

Early one morning I went to the all-night cinema and saw Paloma's film *The Immoral Tales*. I was surprised at how good she was in it. She looked beautiful. She played the queen and her court consisted of young virgins whom she would kill, then bathe in their blood. There were days when I felt as though I were in her court.

As I had suspected, Paloma had been introducing Claude to models at fashion shows while I had been in New York filming *Stepford Wives*. I knew of one beauty that he seemed to fancy who looked like Vivien Leigh.

I left the theatre and went and sat by the pool to read about French history. Maybe Marie Antoinette would have known how to deal with Paloma. Maybe Stanley Loomis's French history books could help me to understand the French.

One day, as I was walking Tutu, a mistral began to blow. My hat fell in my face and my leg ended up in a hole. As I pulled my leg out, I saw the bone, and blood gushing all over my clothing. In shock, I didn't feel a thing. I waved to the *plagist* as though I wanted a *mattelas*. When he looked at my injury, he was horrified. Then I became hysterical. The *plagist* ordered a taxi to take me away. I hadn't been able to grab Tutu at the time, and the last image I had was him running after the cab. As blood ran down my calf onto the taxi's seat, all I could think about was Tutu. Fortunately, he turned out to be OK. The hospital gave me eleven stitches and a prescription for antibiotics, which I was to take as soon as possible. This was about eleven in the morning. When I spoke to Claude, he said he would come to the hotel as soon as possible and bring me the medicine.

At 10 PM that night, he showed up, complaining that he had been forced to find an all-night pharmacy. By that time, I was devastated. The psychological pain was worse than the physical. Claude cared less and less for me. His priorities were obvious.

Back in Paris it was the same thing. During the day Claude was with lawyers while I was left alone, often late into the night.

One day, to pass the time I thought I would go to Maxim's for lunch. Claude hated Maxim's. He told me it was too bourgeois and I was not allowed to go there.

I invited Denise Lindner, who was my only friend in Paris. She and her husband, Richard Lindner, the artist, had been our neighbors in New York for six years. Richard became the uncle of our teacup poodle, Tutu, who understood French. Richard adored Tutu and had frequent conversations with him. The Lindners were fun. In London they had bought a beautiful Bentley and had hired a chauffeur. Denise would drive us to Maxim's in the Bentley, and I would take care of the check.

When Denise and I walked into the restaurant, the maitre d' held out his hands for my beautiful red Jean Muir cape—and for Tutu!

I had not checked the Michelin Guide first. Maxim's was *pas de chien*! I was miserable.

Tutu always dined with Claude and me. He had the *plat du jour*. The idea of Tutu being held captive in a closet while I was feeding my face and trying to be chic made me sick.

I did not enjoy that lunch.

Also I allowed the waiters to intimidate me. I was too frightened to ask the waiter about the dishes as my French was not up to snuff for Chez Maxim's. Or so I felt. So I ordered two dishes that were basically the same thing. And I ordered them because they were among the cheapest items on the menu.

I hated Maxim's. Claude had been right, but I had to find out for myself.

When I returned to our apartment, Claude had found out about my bourgeois luncheon and the "shit hit the fan"--one of his favorite expressions.

Claude was still jealous and used to follow me. Everything I did he wanted to know about and to approve.

One day Sylvie from my therapy group in New York called. She was in Paris. I met her for lunch. I chose the Brasserie Lipp because it was on Claude's "approved" list, and we could always get a nice table there. Out of the blue, Claude appeared for coffee with about twenty questions for Sylvie. I still loved him and thought this meant he cared.

New York, My Kind of Town

One friend whose company I enjoyed was the film producer Jean-Pierre Rassam. I had met Jean-Pierre with my ex-husband in St. Tropez in 1970. By 1974, he had become the head of Gaumont, France's most powerful film distribution company. Jean-Pierre, who was Lebanese, produced *La Grand Bouffe*, directed by Marco Ferreri; *Touche Pas La Femme Blanche*, starring Catherine Deneuve ; and *Chinoise á Paris*, starring Jean Yanne.

Through Jean-Pierre I had met the talented actress and beauty Anna Karina, who was Jean-Luc Goddard's wife, and Roman Polanski, the film director. Roman and I became friends. (In 1975, when I began to date Peter Sellers, Roman was often at his house listening to tapes of the *Goon Show* with Peter and me. Sometime after this Roman and I met at a party in Malibu and he wanted to take me back to my apartment, but I preferred Rip Torn, who drank like I did. Over the years Roman and I would remain in touch and even corresponded. He was thoughtful and read an early draft of my Mailer memoir.)

Jean-Pierre also tried to introduce me to Marcello Mastroianni. In the late seventies Jean-Pierre had arranged for Marcello to take me to the Oscars in Hollywood, but I had unfortunately taken a Quaalude. Alcoholism and addiction were ruling my life and I missed the Oscars that year, but Marcello and I did manage to go on a date soon after.

Jean-Pierre was fun, enjoyed making others laugh, and was a brave, outrageous spirit capable of anything. He drank like I did. Claude drank a lot, but he did not consume the amount of wine that I did at a dinner.

Claude forbade me to see Jean-Pierre, who had introduced me to all these filmmakers and movie people. Claude referred to Jean-Pierre as RassaMMM. Well, that RassMMM was someone I could hang out with during the day while Claude was counting his Picassos. Sometimes I'd sneak out to lunch with Jean-Pierre to La Coupole and not tell Claude. Then I'd feel guilty for deceiving Claude, tell him the truth, and we'd have a huge fight.

One day Claude left for Rome on a business trip for the estate.

"Why can't I come?" I asked.

"You'd be bored and in the way," Claude said. "I'm only going to be gone five days.

"Chérie, please be understanding."

Shortly after Claude dragged his suitcase out of our apartment, the phone rang. "*Allo*," I said.

"What you do, Carolina?" said Jean-Pierre in his gravelly, sexy voice. I should add that he was not good-looking.

"Don't know really. Claude just flew to Rome."

"Without you?"

"Looks that way."

"He's such a bore, really. Your life is going by faster than the Concorde and you sit in that apartment waiting for him to count his paintings."

"I love him, Jean-Pierre."

"Love, love, what is love?"

"You live alone. What do you know about love?"

"Claude's kind of love is making you his prisoner, his hostage."

"I'm here of my own free will."

"HA! He's treating you like his servant. His slave."

"No, he isn't." I opened a bottle of wine.

"And you sit around taking orders from him giving up your freedom."

"Stop it, Jean-Pierre, that's not true."

Picasso's Ghost

"Then come to dinner with me tonight and prove it. I'm meeting Marcello Mastrioanni and Catherine Deneuve."

"You know I can't," I said, hung up, and cried. Jean-Pierre was right. I had become Claude's prisoner. No wonder I hated Paris. It wasn't Paris, though. It was the life I was forced to lead with Claude. Correction: It was the life I was choosing to lead with Claude.

I finished the bottle of wine, polishing it off with a Valium, and passed out.

It was spring of 1975 and *Stepford Wives* was about to be released in the States. My wedding dress was almost two years old and no longer in fashion. My drinking was out of control, as was my frame of mind. Jonas had tried to warn me about the combination of Valium and wine. "It can put you in a coma," Jonas said. "Have you heard of Karen Ann Quinlan? She's in a coma due to alcohol and Valium."

I hadn't heard of Karen Ann Quinlan and didn't care about her, or myself. I needed to knock myself out each night. Sex with Claude was over. Our love had been replaced by Picasso treasures.

I was rich. I could buy anything on credit. So why didn't I feel rich? I know. It was the rain. It was always raining in Paris. Bad weather was always a good reason to drink.

My depression was born out of homesickness. I would call my mother in Valley Forge, Pennsylvania.

"Mom, it's Carole," I said. "Can I speak to Daddy?"

"He's in the hospital," she said "Didn't you get my letter? He tried to commit suicide because of your driver's license."

I became hysterical. "Why didn't you call me?" I said, shouting into the phone. "Where is he?"

"The Lankenau Hospital."

"I'll be home tomorrow." I said, hung up and grabbed a bottle of wine.

Apparently my father wanted to mail my Pennsylvania driver's license to me in Paris. On his way to the nearest mailbox he was stopped by the police. They knew him well and had arranged for his driver's license to be taken away because of the twitching brought on by Parkinson's. Still my father drove. Humiliated, and deciding not to face my mother's wrath, he chose a garage filled with carbon monoxide. He didn't die, but poisonous gases mixed with the scar tissue from the lobotomy, and he became more confused than ever after this event.

I called my therapist in Manhattan.

"My father tried to commit suicide," I said. "Claude is stalling about the wedding date and treating me like his prisoner. I think he has a girlfriend. I am drinking every night and suicide is looking good to me, too."

"Get on the first plane out of there," he said. "Preserve what love he has left for you. Call me when you get in."

I opened the bottle of wine.

When Claude came in from the lawyers, I confronted him. "When are we getting married?"

He was silent.

"Claude, I asked you a question. When are we getting married?"

He was silent.

"My father tried to kill himself. I won't audition to be your wife any longer. I'm leaving on the first plane in the morning."

Claude kicked Tutu, who whimpered and lay in a corner.

"You bastard," I said. "That's what you are. You're doing to me what your father did to your mother!"

Claude slammed his fist into the bathroom wall and kicked Tutu again, who limped into another room.

I began to pack. It was 6 PM. I would have to spend the night there and leave in the morning.

"Let's go to dinner," Claude said with a smirk

He was getting back at me. I always had been the one wanting to go to restaurants and each night had studied the Gault Millau magazine that rated bistros to find a new place to eat. And to drink. A new drink.

Tonight he picked the restaurant. I had lost my appetite. I was drinking my dinner.

He chose a morbid greasy spoon run by Greeks. He consumed a large order of moussaka. Over dinner there was this blankness, with the occasional twinkle in his eyes, as though he really didn't care. Or he was daring me to do as I had threatened.

Picasso's Ghost

After a sleepless night filled with packing and tears, before boarding the plane, I asked," Claude, could I have the $3,000 I lent to you?"

On the way to the airport he stopped at a bank and threw the money at me. "Here, shove it up your cunt," he said.

Tutu and I boarded the first plane and did not look back. Tutu did not whimper when I took him from Claude's arms. I cried the whole way home. I never wanted to return to Paris. (And never have.) At that moment, I could not remember having been this sad. Ever. My world had caved in. Collapsed. My plans of becoming Madame Picasso had disintegrated. What would my father say? He had wanted to be a Rockefeller. I had thought becoming a Picasso was a close second, but I had let down the man I had loved the most. I would be a failure in my father's eyes. In my family's eyes. In my friends' eyes. In all of New York's eyes. Rather than face the humiliation of telling everyone that I had been jilted by Claude, that Claude had refused to set a wedding date and no longer wanted to marry me, I told everyone that I had left him. My ego and my pride ruled. Even during tragedy. Especially during tragedy.

I clutched Tutu and was grateful that I had taken him. How wonderful that he had wanted to come with me. He didn't want to be kicked by Claude anymore, and neither did I. All that money was not worth abuse. I had felt like Claude's slave. The good thing about this whole experience was that I learned being rich does not guarantee happiness. I didn't feel rich. I could have had any material possession I wanted, but I felt poor. I FELT POOR.

Nothing I could have bought would have given me my self-respect, which I regained when I refused the millions that now obscured his love. He had no love. He was in love with power. The false power that money can buy. This false power destroyed all of his loving feelings. My father had tried to kill himself and needed me, but instead of comforting me, Claude drove a stake through my heart by allowing me to go home without asking me to return. Without caring about my father's suffering. He had feigned to care about my father when we had been in love. When Claude needed my money. Now these loving feelings for my father had been buried under bureaucratic red tape. The red tape that surrounded the millions of dollars Claude clawed through life to get to. Would do anything to get to. Even deceive me to get to. Money was not going to rule me. Sure, I would always want more, but not at the price of my dignity, my self-respect, my soul. Finally Tutu and I were home. Safe and together. Never ever again to go to Paris. Ever, ever. My country 'tis of thee. Yes, I was. An American. And grateful through and through.

Françoise Gilot writes in *Life with Picasso*, "For Claude, toys were not something to play with, but something to break. From the age of three on, whenever a new toy came into the house, he would take a hammer and go to work on it, not to see what was inside, as most children want to do, but to reduce it to rubble."

When I returned from Paris, my first stop was to visit my father in the Lankenau Hospital on Philadelphia's main line.

He was in intensive care and didn't know me. The nurses had put him in a straitjacket because he kept ripping the catheter out of his penis. He twitched severely and it was obvious with each movement he was restrained by the jacket, which was cutting into his flesh. The hospital was torturing my father. His eyes blinked uncontrollably and he wore a pasty grin. He didn't recognize me.

"Daddy, it's Carole, your daughter," I said as I held him.

"Oh, that's right. Can you tell them to take this goddamn thing off me?"

"I can't, Daddy. The hospital is in charge and they have rules. They say you rip the catheter out and you can't do that. We want you to get well and to come home. I flew back from Paris just to be with you."

"That was kind of you. I won't take it out. I promise."

"But you told the nurses that before. They said you still do it, Daddy. Now be a good boy. It'll all be over soon. I love you."

"Can you get me a cup of coffee?"

"They don't want you to have that either as it makes you twitch more, but I'll get it and I won't tell them. It will be our secret. I don't want to live in France anymore, Pops. I don't want to marry Claude." I said, lying.

"Good. Now I can see more of you," he said, smiling that lobotomized grin.

We kissed. He didn't understand what I had said. His brain was clouded with carbon monoxide. His sad eyes still wanted me to help him. I couldn't. I hated hospitals and their rules. I hated rules. The hospital didn't have enough nurses to watch my father, and the straitjacket saved them the money they would have had to pay to the necessary staff to safely care for its patients. I left the hospital in tears.

Flying Over the Coo Coo's Nest

All I remember is not being able to get out of bed, but the phone rang in the midst of my tears. Tutu was licking my cheek. It was my wonderful agent, Ruth, who said, "Get up. Get out of bed. I have an audition for you." She didn't ask what had happened. Just gave me courage and support to get on with my life. "It's for *The Fan Club* by Irving Wallace."

It was the spring of 1975 and *Stepford Wives* was about to be released by Columbia, which was also producing *The Fan Club*.

"It's about a sex symbol who's kidnapped by four men," Ruth said, "There's nudity. It's a victim-turned-survivor story. You'd be perfect. Interested?"

"Sure. Why not?" I said, wondering what else I had to do with my life.

"It's the lead. It's been offered to Raquel Welch, Bridget Bardot, Sophia Loren, but since there's nudity, none of these ladies want to do it. Guaranteed to make a sex symbol and star out of the unknown. Let's see if you can nab this one. Knock their socks off on the audition. And stop feeling sorry for yourself. Boring."

I loved Ruth. She did not coddle me, encouraging my self-pity.

Carole Mallory

Columbia Pictures chose me to test for a movie because of this photo

Picasso's Ghost

After walking Tutu and grabbing a quick bite, I took a cab to Columbia's offices on Fifth Avenue. There I met with the short, paunchy English director, John Hough, who fingered an 8x10 glossy of me in a crocheted bikini and asked, "Do you have any objections to nudity?"

"No, only frontal nudity," I said, avoiding his penetrating gaze.

"This is Columbia pictures. You won't have to worry about that."

"What's it about?"

"A sex symbol who's kidnapped by a truck driver, Vietnam vet eran, insurance salesman, and ex-convict. They rape her. She's forced to have sex for survival. She uses her wits to kill three of them and falls in love with the fourth. Can you handle it?" he asked, while gazing into my eyes.

"Yes," I said, thinking, anything to forget Claude. I would show him. I was ready with the necessary anger and rage.

"So far I've met with 1500 women and it's difficult to find sexy, sensual yet classy women." He paused, fingered my photo again, looked out the window and said, "Would you like to read for the part? I'd like to see what you'd bring to the character."

The next day, after leaving Tutu with a kind neighbor, I was on a plane to Hollywood. First class. I celebrated my upcoming test with a fine bottle of red wine.

Columbia booked a suite for me in the Beverly Hills Hotel. There was one other girl from New York, but the studio had stuck her in a motel. What cheek, I thought.

Advertisements had been placed in *The Hollywood Reporter* and *Variety* with a shadowed silhouette of a woman captioned, "Who will star in THE FAN CLUB?" A search had been conducted across America. Only six had been selected to test: Linda Carter, Catherine Bach, Marjorie Wallace (a former Miss America), Barbara Leigh, the poor dear in the motel, and me. With all this hoopla I was beginning to hope the film would never be made.

My tears for Claude were fading and my aspirations of being Madame Picasso had been temporarily replaced with aspirations to being an actress.

Flowers and men began appearing at my door. I was being given the Hollywood rush and was hit on by creeps, creeps, and more creeps. But there were a few twinkling stars.

One day while basking in the sun by the pool (this ritual helped me to forget Claude more than any man), my name was paged over the loudspeaker. I had left a forwarding number on my answering machine at home. The closest phone at the pool happened to be behind a sandbox. I had to stand in this sandbox while my left foot was attacked by a two-year-old with a toy shovel. The child followed my foot as I tried to move away from him.

I answered the phone.

"This is Jack..."

"Jack who?" I asked, wondering whose low purring voice this was.

"Jack Nicholson. Heard you were in town and wondered if you'd have tea with me today around 4?"

God, he was direct, I thought as the two-year-old pounded my pinky toe.

We had, in fact, met on the night of Jacqueline Onassis's anniversary while I was on a date with Mike Nichols, but that was several years ago.

"Jack, we haven't seen each other for years."

"You're hard to forget," Jack said. I could imagine his mischievous smile. His voice, laden with sensuality.

"I have plans this afternoon. What about dinner tonight?" I asked, thinking, if he can be this aggressive why can't I?

Though I'd met Jack a few times after that, this was even a bit forward for him, but I was flattered. I'd had a tremendous crush on him because in *One Flew over the Cuckoo's Nest* he reminded me of my father.

"I'm down here at the Hotel Biltmore filming *The Last Tycoon* and can only squeeze in tea at your place some afternoon," he said in a whisper. "My schedule's just too hectic at night. You know how that is."

WHATTHEFUCK, I thought, quoting Claude in my head. Jack may have reminded me of my father, but my father would never have treated me so shabbily. "I really like you, Jack," I said. "But unless you take me to dinner, I cannot allow myself to be with you. Are you ashamed to be seen with me in public?"

The two-year-old hacked at my heel. I pulled the phone cord as far away from him as possible, suppressing my desire to hit him—since I couldn't hit Jack.

"It's not that," Jack said in his signature velveteen voice, "But this is a small town. You'll see People talk. I keep very private and like it that way."

"I wouldn't feel good about myself if I agreed to your terms"

"You don't understand." His voice became harsh. "I can't be seen with you." Jack Nicholson was in a committed relationship with Angelica Huston.

"Jack, you can't just come over for tea."

"Why not?" His voice became seductive. Sneaky.

"I don't really know you."

"Let's get to know each other."

"Really, Jack, I'd love to get to know you over dinner."

"Can't do that."

"Then I can't be tea."

"Please?"

"How did you get my number?"

"A mutual friend."

"Jack, please take me to dinner."

"Not possible."

"Goodbye, Jack," I hung up on Jack Nicholson.

The small child had hacked at my foot throughout the conversation. I scowled at him and stepped out of the sandbox. That's what Jack had wanted me to be--his sandbox.

Jack Nicholson never called again.

The day of the *Fan Club* test was approaching. One afternoon a fitting was arranged in my suite of the Beverly Hills Hotel. My director, John Hough, wanted to select one of my swimsuits for the test. At his request I tried on a variety of bikinis. Finally he picked his favorite, never once making a pass. John Hough was supportive of my work and I felt safe with him considering the nature of the film and of my part.

It was the day of the test. I had filmed four of my scenes. Using Claude's photo as motivation for my anger, with blanks I shot actor Adam Rourke in his crotch. I wondered what Claude was doing with his life? Dealing with the estate, no doubt, while I was dealing with Hollywood.

We were moving to the final bedroom scene. I was told to prepare, which meant to undress. Standing on the side of the set, I wrapped a blanket around me.

Director Hough stepped into the spotlight and assertively said, "Carole, please stand by the bed, drop the blanket, and lie with your back on the bed."

WHAT?! I signaled that I wanted to talk with director Hough.

"John, you told me in New York that this scene would be shot with my tummy on the bed, and now you tell me the opposite?"

"All the other actresses have done it, Carole," director Hough said, calmly. "If you want to be considered for the part, you must do the scene this way."

"I told you in New York I would not do frontal nudity and you agreed."

"It's a requirement of the producer. I have no control in this matter."

"Can I speak with the producer?" I asked, clutching my blanket.

"Larry Gordon is in Texas completing a film. These tests will be stored in Columbia's vault. No one will see them except the persons making the decision."

Oh God! I thought.

"This is a prestigious film, Carole, dealing with exploitation and victimization. The intention of these tests is to create a star, not victimize actresses. Victimization is what this film is about."

Director Hough explained this to me in an earnest, sincere manner. Previously he had directed a film for Disney. He seemed so genuine that I felt I had to believe him. Besides, he had made it clear that I had no choice if I wanted to be cast in this film.

I had to make a new life. I was going to survive Claude's rejection. I would have done almost anything to forget Claude. I dropped the blanket.

Picasso's Ghost

As I lay on the bed, handcuffs were put on each wrist then my wrists were separated and attached to opposite ends of the bedposts. The crucifixion pose. My back was raised on pillows so that my breasts fell in a perfect position for camera.

This scene was about photographing a pair of breasts. I had crossed my feet at the ankles. The camera was off to the right at the base of the bed, which meant that if I raised my legs, my most private part would be filmed.

I wasn't going to unlock my legs. I lay there handcuffed and cross-legged trying to forget and to deny what I was doing. I wanted to believe the director. He had been nice to me and had never come on to me. I had to believe someone.

Oh, where was Claude? Then I remembered he had once assisted a director in making porno films. How could he have done that? He wouldn't have helped me. He would have helped the director. Claude. Claude victimized me. That's why I was thinking about Claude.

Now director Hough gently gave his direction. "Adam Rourke is going to come in from offstage and grab your stomach and you are going to imagine that he is raping you. You may kick, scream, whatever you like to free yourself from this bondage."

This bondage was Hollywood.

I wasn't going to fight any more. It was clear that if I uncrossed my legs to kick or moved in the slightest, the camera would film between my legs.

I couldn't think again about this lousy Goddamn scene.

YES! I was being victimized.

And YES, I was allowing it. I was being raped by Hollywood.

I wondered what Marilyn Monroe had had to do to become a star?

I thought manipulation and control were part of loving and caring. If you do this for me and say YES, you will get that—LOVE and the part.

And so YES became my middle name. I became the embodiment of the casting couch. My sexuality was about to become a cavernous monster and eat up half of Hollywood as well as swarms of curious men wanting a taste while I swallowed my self-respect.

I would hurt myself by allowing these men to do to me what they wanted to do. When I had never wanted to be with them at all. Drinking would help me to achieve my depraved goal. When I drank I could have had sex with the Hunchback of Notre Dame, the Elephant Man, or a leper.

I was going to show Claude how far I could go! How outrageous I could be! How I didn't need him! How he couldn't control me! How much I was like his mother and father. Or so my ego wanted to believe. I wanted to get back at Claude for not marrying me, for allowing me to leave.

By saying YES to the demands of the test, I had given my power to the men who had ordered it and had become their victim. This had been my fault. I had no one to blame but myself.

When the test was over, I returned to the Beverly Hills Hotel in a limousine hired by the studio, ran to my room, fell on my bed, and cried. I was so ashamed. What would my parents think of me if they knew what I had done? This would kill them. Well, I wasn't going to let it kill me. I ordered a bottle of Dom Perignon on Columbia and soon passed out.

The next day I awakened holding the empty champagne bottle and wearing the same faded jeans. A tremendous headache overpowered me. I had trouble remembering the day before. That was fine. Just fine.

That night I had a drink with the director. "Your test was excellent, Carole. I'm very pleased with your performance. You have a good chance for the part."

While awaiting the results of the tests, I spent most of my time by the beautiful, sunny, hotel pool where one day I met the English director, Nicholas Roeg who was most known for directing *Walkabout* and *Don't look Now*. Terribly witty in that wonderful British manner, Nick enjoyed drinking as much as I did. We became friends and lovers. Nick made me feel special and not sexually inadequate as I had grown to feel with Claude.

One night I introduced Nick, who had been a cinematographer, to John Hough. We had cocktails in the Polo Lounge. Suddenly John asked Nick, "Which half of *Lawrence of Arabia* did you photograph?" I didn't understand John Hough's hostility.

Two days later John Hough was fired from directing *The Fan Club* and replaced by Nick Roeg. James Poe was to rewrite the abysmal script. I was thrilled.

John Hough had told me that it had been between Linda Carter and me.

Nick Roeg was a prestigious director, which meant the film was guaranteed to be quality.

After two weeks at the Beverly Hills Hotel, I moved to a girl friend's flat in West Hollywood. One night we were invited to a party for Charlotte Rampling, who was starring in a film about to be released. This was to be a big Hollywood extravaganza. I decided to wear the dress I'd worn in one of my *Fan Club* test scenes. It was a black Christian Dior I'd bought in Paris while awaiting my wedding to Claude. Claude had hated this dress because it showed too much cleavage. Wearing it was getting back at Claude.

When my girlfriend and I arrived at the party, we fought our way through agents, stars, managers to get to the bar. A bearded, good-looking gentleman stared at me.

"I'm Larry Gordon, your producer," he said, sternly, with a slight twinkle in his eyes.

Why, he was the producer of *The Fan Club*. He was handsome, yet nervous and insecure. Suddenly he seemed antagonistic toward me. Was it because I was a New Yorker? New Yorkers were not liked by Hollywood folk.? Or was it because he was ashamed because he had demanded screen tests designed to film the breasts and pubic areas of five aspiring actresses?

"Hello, Larry. How was Texas?" I asked, not knowing what else to say.

An entourage seemed to form around him. I was not introduced to anyone. Someone in the group asked if we'd ever met. Our awkwardness was apparent.

"No, I've never met Carole," he said, trying to exude an air of authority. There was a down-home charm to Larry, but to overcome his insecurities and this sweetness, he seemed to act tough.

"No, I didn't pick Carole to test," he said. "She was the choice of the director, John Hough. I'd only seen a photo of her." He kept talking about me in the third person as though I weren't there.

"Well, Carole," he said, smiling. "I'm sorry to tell you this, but you won't be starring in *The Fan Club*. Your tits are too small and you're too classy. Sorry."

Quickly I left the party.

I didn't remember driving home, and passed out in my bed.

A few weeks later it was announced that Nick Roeg was going to have total control over the female lead in *The Fan Club*. Larry Gordon's choice of the film's star had been taken away from him. Nick and Larry had opposite tastes. Nick was European and had tremendous style and heart.

Since *The Fan Club* had received so much hype and everyone was awaiting the emergence of a new sex symbol, I became a mini *cause célèbre*. I was invited to parties, parties and more parties and loved it. Claude was becoming a memory.

An old modeling friend from New York, Alana Collins, who had married the actor George Hamilton and later Rod Stewart and had become quite the Hollywood wife and hostess.

One afternoon she invited me to my first A-list luncheon at her home on San Ysidro Drive. I didn't know which door to enter so I walked in the front door and almost stumbled on Alana, who said, "Oh, Carole, please use the kitchen door. George is trying to sell this house and this white carpet will be black in two seconds if all the guests walk on it." Plastic covered part of the white wall-to-wall and made a nice, neat runway through to the backyard. But Alana preferred me to enter through the kitchen.

A woman wearing a black-and-white maid's outfit asked if I wanted something to drink. Later I was told this woman was Alana's mother.

Alana whispered, "Why are you late? Everyone's here. Sometimes I worry about you. Were you fucking Nick last night?"

"I'm hung over. That's why I'm late."

"Honestly, Carole, why do you drink like you do? Pull yourself together. I want you to meet Dani and David Janssen, Joan Collins, Raquel Welch, and Karen and Michael Callan. That's who's here so far. And stay away from the men! Make friends with the women. That's who runs Hollywood."

As we walked out of the kitchen into the pool area, I saw these Hollywood celebrities seated on the hillside at the far end of a beautiful Moorish pool.

I became nervous. "Where's the bar, Alana?"

"Really, Carole, I thought you were hung over?"

"The best thing for a hangover is a drink."

"Sure," Alana said, grimacing. "George has made a pitcher of margaritas."

I was introduced to the group on the hill, then returned to the pool, quickly took off the robe covering my bikini and dove in. I couldn't stand all the social small talk, even though I wanted so badly to be a part of it. Talking to people, especially celebrities, made me feel uncomfortable unless I had a drink in my hand.

George Hamilton was paddling around the pool with his son, Ashley. "You look ravishing today, Carole."

"You're just saying that, George. I feel terrible. Too much to drink last night. Up too late."

As I reached the middle of the pool, I overheard Raquel Welch laughing. She was covered in a white caftan from head to toe on a hot summer day. She was amused by something.

"Well, there I was in the middle of Peter Guber's living room last night watching the tests of this film, *The Fan Club*. In the midst of the madness Peter had the sick sense of humor to show these six girls on film on his giant screen. They were naked, chained to a bed. Their legs in the air. I thought, 'Don't these girls have any shame?' It's amazing what starlets will do today to become a sex symbol." She laughed.

I ran to the kitchen for another margarita. I never found out if Raquel Welch had known I had been one of these women. This didn't seem to be the issue. After I downed the margarita, I slipped out of Alana's home through the kitchen door. When I returned to my apartment, I tore up a photo of Claude and passed out in my bed.

After all this Hollywood hoopla and publicity, *The Fan Club* was never made.

Nick Roeg refused to direct it. He wanted explicit nudity, like the smash film of the moment, *Emmanuele*, but Columbia Pictures wanted an R rating on an X-rated story. This didn't make sense to Nick.

Or to me. But then nothing about *The Fan Club* had ever made sense.

Years later Norman Mailer said, "Sounds like someone was ripping off Columbia."

The best thing to come from my *Fan Club* experience was an agent. John Gaines, of the Agency of the Performing Arts, had seen my test and wanted to sign me.

"If you want to work as a film actress, you must live in Hollywood. Then I'll sign you."

I liked his words. I thought John Gaines believed in me as an actress. I had found a reason to leave New York.

Within days I flew back to the Sovereign and returned to Hollywood with Tutu and most of my clothing. The Chateau Marmont accepted dogs. I left my furniture and paintings in New York and moved to the Chateau until I found an apartment.

Claude and I had a lease at the Sovereign until 1977, but what was I going to do? Sit around that gorgeous apartment and mope over him? If he wanted me, he was going to have to find me and to treat me right.

Los Angelenos take the sun for granted and never sit in it. They look at it and hide from it. But my East Coast corpuscles, frozen from days of forging ahead through rain, snow, and sleet, took to the sun like a junkie to heroin. The warm, loving sun seemed temporarily to heal my pain and anger.

Taxi Driver

When I first moved to Hollywood in 1975, for a few months I stayed in the Chateau Marmont. It was sleepy, sensual, mysterious and in 1982 would be the scene of John Belushi's death in one of its bungalows from a heroin overdose. Robin Williams and Bobby DeNiro had left Belushi at about 3 AM, noticing he was ill, and were the last to see him alive. A cool, hip hotel, the Chateau was known for its rock n' roll clientele and stars who wanted privacy, I had booked a room on its fourth floor for Tutu and myself. We were the stars of the fourth floor because we had a refrigerator in my closet. Mart Crowley, who wrote *The Boys in the Band*, lived a few doors down, and we hung out with his friend, Nick Dunne, who visited us on occasion.

One night after leaving my room, I stepped into the elevator. A man slouched in the corner with a tam over one eye. He resembled a garage mechanic. He stared at me. The elevator door closed. "Are you a guest here?" he asked.

"No, I live with my dog on the fourth floor."

"So do I. No dog."

We were passing the third floor.

I recognized the voice. The sly smile.

"What's your name?" he asked.

"Carole Mallory," I said.

"I'm Bobby De Niro," he said. "Are you a New Yorker?"

Oh, My, God! I thought. "Yes, just moved here."

We were passing the second floor.

He took off his hat, stood up and studied my eyes. "You look like a New Yorker." Bobby was smaller than I expected, but he had that earthy sex appeal he exuded on screen. "We're a rare breed out here," he said with a chuckle.

"I've noticed," I said, trying to hide my nervousness. "Do you miss New York?"

"I only come to L.A. when I'm paid. Do you want to have a drink later?" he asked.

"Sure," I said. "I'll be back about 11."

"Me, too, I have to meet a director," he said. "How about if I knock on your room about 11? What's your room number?"

"402. That would be great," I said, while wondering, "What Claude would think?"

The elevator had arrived at the garage. We went our separate ways. I was stunned. Bobby De Niro moved fast. I met Bobby on the fourth floor and by the first floor I had a date for that night at 11.

Berry and Tony Perkins had invited me to dinner that night. Because they had two small children, they ate early.

"Berry, you'll never guess who I met in the elevator." I said, as I walked into their home.

"No idea."

"Bobby De Niro."

"ARE YOU SERIOUS? Did you make a date?"

"Yes, for tonight at 11."

"Well, let's eat and run, then. Tony! Dinner's ready," Berry shouted.

Rarely am I on time, but this night I returned by 10:30 PM to freshen up.

At 10:45 there was a light knock on my door. I opened it to see Bobby De Niro slouching in my doorway wearing that sideways smile.

"Come in," I said.

Bobby entered slowly. "My meeting was shorter than expected," he said.

"Do you want something to drink?" I asked.

"No, thanks. Just a glass of water." Bobby stood, hands in pockets of his faded jeans, and stared into my eyes.

"What movie are you filming?"

"*Bogart Slept Here*."

"How's it going?"

"Problems. That's why we had the meeting."

There was only one chair in the room, a coffee table, and a bed.

"Mind if I sit down?" He sat on the bed. "These things are terrible, aren't they?" he said, as he patted the mattress indicating that I sit by his side.

"Are you all Italian?" I asked.

"Part Italian, German, Dutch. French ...a mixture, but mostly Italian. I was raised by my grandfather, who was Italian."

"What happened to your father?" I asked.

"He left my mother when I was born."

"Why?"

"You ask a lot of questions."

"I want to know you."

"After I was born, my father announced he was a homosexual."

"After I divorced, my husband announced he was a homosexual. Then he became bisexual."

"Small world," Bobby said, smiling.

"Is that why you like to play psychos?"

"Aren't you being presumptuous?"

"Trying to get to know you."

"I don't like to talk it away."

"What do you mean?"

"I like to do it."

"You mean shoot the scene?"

"I mean.." He took my wineglass away from me, placed it on the coffee table, put his arms around me, and kissed me. His lips were sensual, lingering, promising more. I loved the mole on his cheek. He reminded me of French royalty. All he needed was a ruffled shirt and a white wig with ringlets. But he was too down-to-earth to be French nobility—though he could act any character he chose.

Bobby began to undress me as he stared into my eyes. He was studying my face, my character. Undressing me with his eyes as well as his hands. Doing research? Who knew? During lovemaking he never stopped looking into my eyes. I was forgetting about Claude and this felt good.

Bobby's skin was almost white like milk. That had been his nickname—Bobby Milk. I could see why.

He liked me on top of him. A voyeur. But of course. Always studying humanity. He didn't speak. I felt as though I were with a silent film star. Bobby De Niro would have made a good Valentino. His body was taut, spry, agile, almost bony. His finest assets were his firm body and piercing eyes. He had a butterfly tattoo that I later realized matched his flighty spirit. So did the fact that he left his socks on.

I felt his tenderness and a gentle side that he did not like to show. Someone was hidden deep inside and did not want to come out unless he felt safe enough. He was beyond shy. Shy was focused on self. He was focused on everything around him. Taking it all in. Like he was a member of the CIA. He investigated life and sex. So he was not shy.

He looked at all parts of my body. I felt like he was my doctor. I did not fight his requests. It was difficult for him to speak. I knew this. So I had to allow him a long lead. No questions. Well, few questions. I wanted to know whom I was making love to, and though he was trying to hide his soul from me this did not mean I couldn't look for it. Searching, just as he did when he researched characters. I would try to do to Bobby what he did to characters when he wanted to portray them. Like his Method technique of studying his characters' backgrounds, I would try to dig deep into Bobby to find who was there. Someone who was hiding. Someone who was afraid to reveal who he was. He had been hurt. Badly. Childhood was a bummer. A father who had left home and become a homosexual. What had that done to Bobby's identity? Masculinity? Ability to trust? Trust was not part of this man. Maybe under all the layers he could trust a director--a man--with whom he had a proven relationship, but to trust a woman? Maybe a mothering type. His mother had raised him. She had been an artist and a writer who was part of a group that included Henry Miller and Anais Nin. They wrote pornography for a collector. His father was an artist. Abstract Expressionist. Silently expressive in a violent way.

Bobby liked to portray violent characters. His father's artwork had been violent.

Silently violent. Bobby's trademark was to portray brutal characters. Why? Deep within he had such tumult, and when he had an orgasm, he had a primitive release. His anger with being abandoned by his father was all over his being, but deep within. "People don't show their feelings," he would say. "They hide from them."

What was he hiding from? The pain of rejection? Too simplistic? Maybe not. Fear of intimacy. For certain. If someone were to get close to him, he could be abandoned him. Like his father abandoned him.

Mother figures were the safest, but he was not attracted sexually to them. He sought the sultry seductresses. He liked an African-American woman. Then he enjoyed dismissing her. Tossing her to the spectators.

Next?

A white woman, I was an exception to his choice in lovers. I lasted fourteen days.

For two weeks we continued our relationship. For two weeks I was free of haunting thoughts about Claude. Bobby and I could see each other's rooms from our windows. When my light was on, Bobby would knock on my door. He would come in. We would talk briefly and we would make love. Then he would say, "Really, I've got to work on my lines. I've got to rehearse, make choices. I'm only as good as my choices."

"Can I help you?" I asked, caressing his back, which felt warm and cuddly.

"We're having trouble on the film. My director, Mike Nichols, doesn't think I'm funny." Bobby kissed me gently, then pulled away as he reached for his jeans.

"I think you could do anything, Bobby. I saw you in your Brian De Palma's *Hi Mom*. You were very funny, but I understand your need to study. I have to work on my lines for *Brave New World*. They're making it into a TV movie. Have to begin shooting in two days."

"People don't understand how hard acting is," he said. "The good part is it allows us to live other people's lives without paying the price. Movies are hard work. People don't see that. It's working in the middle of the night. It's freezing. You gotta do this scene. You gotta get it to this point." Bobby was pulling on his jeans.

"Do you enjoy watching your performances?" I asked.

"I fall asleep watching my own movies. No, I don't. I enjoy making love to you,"

he said and pulled off his jeans, throwing them on the floor.

Our bodies and souls intertwined for another interlude. Until after two weeks it was over.

One day, without saying goodbye, Bobby moved out of the Chateau. I felt dismissed by him as I moved into my new apartment in a Chinese pagoda-style apartment that had been belonged to Valentino on La Cienega Boulevard in West Hollywood. I realized that Bobby had been going through a tough time when a few weeks later I read in the trades that he had been fired by Mike Nichols, who felt Bobby couldn't handle comedy. Bobby had been replaced by Richard Dreyfuss and the film had been renamed *The Goodbye Girl*. It was the story of what happened to Dustin Hoffman after he became a star. Herbert Ross replaced Mike Nichols, who did not return to Hollywood for a long time, and after him Neil Simon was then at the helm. The film *Bogart Slept Here* had been a disaster as originally cast and never had been filmed. When I met Bobby, the cast was having readings. It was a terrible time for Bobby De Niro. The following year he married Diahnne Abbott. He never spoke of her when we were together, so I had not known he was in a relationship. Superstars' sex lives are usually common knowledge in Hollywood. I should have been more aware of his status. Nevertheless, I would have appreciated a phone call from him.

But I was again consumed with thoughts of Claude Picasso and just exactly what he was doing in Paris. Was he with other women?

Inspecting Clouseau

No word from Claude yet.

One day in the spring of 1975 while hanging out at the pool of the Beverly Hills Hotel looking for fellow New Yorkers, I ran into Bruce Jay Friedman, the handsome author of hit plays such as *Steambath* and movies like *Stir Crazy*. That night Bruce invited me to be his date at a party given by the producer Marty Ransohoff.

As we pulled into the semicircular driveway of Marty's red brick Bel-Air home that evening, Bruce spotted the car of Stan Dragotti, at the time Cheryl Tieg's boyfriend, who would go on to direct *Love at First Bite*. "I've been trying to get in touch with Stan. Great!" Bruce chuckled. "I've saved a quarter."

A tuxedoed waiter opened the door, checked our coats, and escorted us into the very modest but comfortable living room. Immediately, Stan and Cheryl came running over. "What a nice party ol' Marty is givin'," Bruce drawled in his slow but sure Hopalong-Friedman manner. "Gee, isn't that Jackie Bisset over there?"

Stan laughed. "I'll introduce you to her later. First I want you to meet Peter Sellers."

"I'm a big fan of his," Bruce said. "That'd be great! Inspector Clouseau is here? Right now?"

"He's our neighbor. He rented a home on San Ysidro Drive while working on *Murder by Death* for Ray Stark."

"Ah, Neil Simon at work again," Bruce said. "Well, where's Dr. Strangelove? I want to meet him."

"I'll get him. Don't go away. Carole, I think you'll really like Peter. He's available. So if he's your type, give a wink. We're good friends." Stan said, smiling in a fatherly fashion.

Stan and Cheryl went to find Peter.

"Well, Bruce, this is one of 'those parties.' Thanks for inviting me."

"Why, the pleasure's mine, my dear. Look, there's Roman Polanski."

"They're all here," I said. "Isn't that Freddie Fields?"

"None other than."

"I need a drink," I said, nervously.

When we approached the bar, I felt someone tapping my elbow.

"Carole, this is Peter Sellers," Stan said, smiling.

"Hello," I said, as I turned and stared into Peter's sad eyes. They seemed covered in a haze, but worse yet, they were uninterested in me.

"Very nice to me you, Carole," said one of history's greatest comedic artists.

"And this is Bruce Jay Friedman," Stan said.

"Hello, Bruce," Peter said, self-consciously.

"Peter, I'm a great fan of yours."

"Well, thank you. I've read some of your work and enjoy it very much also." Peter looked agitated. "Sorry to be so abrupt, but would you excuse me? I'm going to get some fresh air. It's a bit close in here, wouldn't you say?" Then Peter walked alone into the garden. He looked nervous and quite uncomfortable.

People had been clinging to him, laughing at his straight lines, and wanting him to perform. Peter probably was fed up with Hollywood parties. Understanding him still didn't help my damaged ego.

I was sure Stan had said nice things about me. Why hadn't Peter made more of an effort?

"That was some conversation, Bruce. What's wrong with us?"

"Nothing, dear. That's the price of fame. He probably wants to be alone."

"So why come to a party?"

"Don't ask me these complicated questions, Carole. Peter is probably a serious comedian like most of them. And that's O.K."

I liked Bruce. He always saw the good in people and accepted the little quirks we all have.

"I need another drink," I said, mumbling into an empty glass.

"Well, have one, my dear."

I felt a tap on my elbow. It was Stan. "Well, how did it go with Peter? I'm sorry I had to run away like that."

"He was very nice and very uninterested in me."

Stan looked bewildered.

"What can I tell you? I think it's a pass. Don't worry about it. I'll still go to his movies," I said, feeling rejected.

"Carole, give him another chance. Don't feel like that. He's a shy man and people have been making him feel uptight. It's a lot of pressure to be a comedian, be invited to a party, and be expected to be funny and perform. He's a lovely, sweet man. Why don't we go out into the garden and listen to him? He's out there with Roman and looks comfortable. Polanski's like his son."

"Where's Bruce?"

"Don't worry about him. He'll find us. Besides, I'm sure he'd like to check out the party on his own. You're both just friends, aren't you?"

"That's right," I said, looking down at my wineglass. "Thanks."

We wandered outside and sat in the courtyard. It was a warm summer's night and romance was in the air.

"Peter and Roman, this is Carole Mallory," Stan said.

"How beautiful you are in the moonlight, Miss Mallory," Peter said, smiling. "It is Miss is it not?"

"For now, yes," I said.

Roman stood up and kissed my hand in a mock courtly manner.

"What brings you to this event?" Peter asked.

"The 'who' is my friend, Bruce. The 'what' is probably the same 'what' that brought you."

Peter laughed. "Ah, but aren't you being a bit presumptuous?"

"Why not? I'm wearing pink!"

"That's a good reason. I see your point! Stan told me you are a bit unusual, aside from your beauty. You must be a Capricorn."

"How did you know?" I asked.

"My dear, I believe in astrology and the spirits. I'm a Virgo, myself."

"I dominate you."

"I think I'd like that. When?"

I began to laugh. Peter was fun. Roman, who had been watching, was having trouble sitting still. He had been so happy to be exchanging stories with Peter.

Roman piped up. "Later, later, you two. We were in the middle of something. Peter, go on! What happened after you bought the fireworks?"

"Yes, yes, well, last Fourth of July, I was a guest on Sam Spiegel's yacht in the South of France and we were on the bay of St.-Jean-Cap-Ferrat. The *Malahne* was anchored in front of David Niven's home. I dressed in an old German army officer's uniform and announced over the loudspeaker in a German accent that we were about to torpedo the harbor." Peter stood on a chair and saluted. "WIR IST GOING ZU BOMB ZIZ PORT CAP FERRAT IN ZEHN MINUTEN ...GUTEN TAG, MINE KINDER..."

Peter sat down, chuckling. "Well, there were foghorns, sirens, fireworks, and a huge smokescreen. Sam had arranged it all for the Fourth of July. But the Frogs don't know a bloody thing about that holiday. People were running out of their homes to see what the hell was going on. Ah, it was a sight!" Peter was laughing so hard that he was almost in tears. Roman was holding his belly.

"Then when we saw the sirens from the squad cars and flashing lights, I got back on the loudspeaker and announced in the King's English that we would be pleased to accept Mr. Niven's luncheon invitation. We all had a great laugh at lunch, but the police weren't too amused."

Of all the guests listening Peter and Roman were laughing the hardest and reminded me of two kids playing hooky. Peter loved pranks and loved to laugh. Frequently he would break up in the middle of his own stories and kill his own jokes. Then there were

Picasso's Ghost

times when he would laugh so hard that he would forget what he was saying and repeat, "My, my, now where was I?" Recalling funny situations made him happy. Laughter was his favorite orgasm.

Roman loved Peter and Peter loved Roman. They had worked together in *The Magic Christian*.

"Tell us some Stanley Kubrick stories," Roman asked.

"Oh, you know, I'm not too comfortable at this gathering. I feel I'm on the Hollywood local at rush hour. Would you all like to come back to my home? I have some tapes of Spike Mulligan, Harry Secombe, and myself from the early *Goon Shows*. Do you remember them from the fifties?"

I didn't, but Peter explained it was a radio show on which he enjoyed his first real success. The show was outrageous and bizarre and became a cult in London. I felt Peter was happiest when he didn't care what people were thinking, but unfortunately he had to be performing a character to enjoy these feelings.

The satirical comedy of the *Goons* was anti-establishment, anarchic, and "fuck-the-Joneses." We listened to the episodes where the *Goons* conquer Mt. Everest from the inside, and the one about the donation and installment proceedings of London's Albert Memorial to—and on—the moon.

While listening to the *Goon* tapes, I thought how much Claude would have liked to have been here. He worshipped Peter Sellers just as I had. When I was in middle school, a group of us would go to the Green Hill Movie Theatre on the Main Line to watch Peter's early British films, the ones made before he had been "Hollywoodized."

Peter hated Hollywood parties—the hypocrisy and the hustling. His favorite kind of evening was spent with his cronies playing tricks on the Hollywood establishment or listening to tapes of the *Goons*. Peter was an Englishman through and through—clubby, insular and mistrustful of anything that wasn't English, too.

Some people feel he didn't get the Oscar for *Being There* because of the catty things he'd been saying for years about the town and the industry. In fact, Peter wasn't happy with the films he had made in Hollywood. In an attempt to make amends, around Oscar time Peter took an ad out in *Variety* declaring his only criticism of

Hollywood was as a place to work. This doubletalk did not impress the industry, and Peter was subsequently passed over at the Oscars.

Our first night together, Peter confessed that he hated living in a place with such lousy values—morally and artistically—and began to reminisce about the films he made in London in the 60s. These were the films I had seen as a teenager on Philadelphia's Main Line—classics like *The Lady Killers* and *I'm All Right, Jack*. Peter felt this was some of his best work, along with the *Goon Show*. These roles were done before the money and the fame. The money did come and the celebrity, but not the happiness he craved. I think sometimes Peter felt he was *The Magic Christian* himself. A Magic Christian was someone solely concerned with material gain--the personification of greed. I would have felt like a Magic Christian if I had stayed with Claude and accepted his shabby treatment of me in exchange for his fortune.

From this night on, Peter and I laughed together for almost a year.

Peter was sad a lot of the time and I tried to make him smile. I felt I could make Peter feel better about himself. I had been trying to do this for Claude, too, because Picasso had been so cruel to him. I had a pattern of seeking out men to rescue. It never worked. I couldn't rescue Peter, who wanted to be someone else. I knew my need to rescue came from my feelings of helplessness when I was a child, when I had been unable to do anything to prevent my father's suffering.

Peter and Claude reminded me of each other. I felt both suffered from depression, and sought relief through laughter. So did my father. Maybe we all do, but we can't all create humor as Peter could. Claude also tried to be funny by imitating Charlie Chaplin in his movements—because his father had emulated Chaplin. Claude enjoyed making hand gestures like Chaplin, mimicking his performances in silent films.

Pablo Picasso had admired Charlie Chaplin and had identified in a symbolic way with circus performers, in that they, too, were solitary performers like artists. The acrobats and tumblers he etched in the *Saltimbanques* series. Or the matadors whose struggles he made his own and whose drama he seemed to carry over into almost every phase of his life and his art.

The clown, too, was one of the most tragic yet heroic figures in the circus. Claude would tell me that almost every morning as Pablo lathered his face for shaving, he would trace with his finger in the billowing cream the enormous caricatured lips, the suggestions of question marks over the eyebrows, and the path of tears oozing out of each eye—the stigmata of the professional clown.

"Why do you do that, Papa?" Claude told me he would ask Picasso who would begin to gesticulate and grimace with an intensity that showed this was not only a game, but his attempt to imitate Charlie Chaplin.

"I loved being my father's audience and watching him in front of the mirror as he talked to himself made up like a clown," Claude said. "I would sit on the floor and laugh as Françoise would come into the room and join in."

Like Claude listening to his father, I would sit in the kitchen of Peter Sellers's home and be his audience as he rehearsed his lines, using funny expressions for my teacup poodle, Tutu, and me. Unlike Claude I did not laugh, but remained quiet so as not to disturb Peter's concentration.

Claude continued to talk about Picasso. "My father had been an avid fan of Chaplin during the silent film days, but when the talkies came along my father lost all interest in movies. When *Monsieur Verdoux* was announced, he could not contain his excitement in seeing this film. For my father, Chaplin's art was the embodiment of the physical stylization of his 'little man' role.'"

It has been written that after seeing *Verdoux*, Pablo cherished those scenes where Chaplin relied on mime to produce his effects. Those scenes, where Chaplin flipped through the pages of the telephone directory and over and over again counted money, were responsible for the way Picasso counted or miscounted money. The direct force of the film image seemed to duplicate the kind of shock that comes when one looks at a painting, Picasso said.

"It's the same thing, to the extent that you work on the senses to convey your meaning," Picasso is said to have noted about Chaplin.

"Mime is the exact equivalent of the gesture in painting by which you transmit directly a state of mind—no description, no analysis, no words."

I believed Peter Sellers would have had an interesting discussion with Picasso about comedy and Peter's dislike of improvisation. When Peter had helped me with a script, he had told me I had to set my gestures, my tone of voice, and my accent. I had to set everything. "An actor is only as good as her or his choices," Peter had said.

Picasso had wanted to meet Chaplin because, he said, "He's a man who like me has suffered a great deal at the hands of women." Chaplin had serious relationships with thirteen women.

I believed Peter Sellers, who had a complicated history with women, would have enjoyed talking to Picasso about this. And what about Norman Mailer, who decapitated women in his fiction, stabbed them in real life, and had a total of six wives. How wonderful it would have been to have interviewed Charlie Chaplin, Peter Sellers, and Norman Mailer about women!

Claude went on to tell me that in 1952, Picasso finally did have the opportunity to meet Chaplin after the French premiere of *Limelight*. They met in Pablo's studio in the rue des Grand Augustins, but Chaplin did not speak French and Picasso did not speak English. Interpreters were hired, but they proved to be in the way.

Then Picasso had the idea to take Chaplin upstairs away from the crowd so that they could be alone and establish some kind of communication. "I took Chaplin upstairs to my painting studio and showed him the pictures I had been working on." Picasso has said. "When I finished, I gave him a bow and a flourish to let him know it was his turn. He understood at once. He went into the bathroom and gave me the most wonderful pantomime of a man washing and shaving, with every one of those little involuntary reflexes like blowing the soapsuds out of his nose and digging them out of his ears. When he had finished that routine, he picked up two toothbrushes and performed that marvelous dance with the rolls, from the New Year's Eve dinner in *The Gold Rush*."

But Picasso objected to the sentimentality of *Limelight*. "I don't like that maudlin, sentimentalizing side of Chaplin," he said. "That's for shopgirls, when Chaplin starts reaching for the heart strings. Maybe Chaplin impresses Chagall, but it doesn't go down with me. It's just bad literature."

I wondered what Picasso would have thought of Peter Sellers's performance in the classic *Being There*. So many people felt Peter deserved the Oscar for his performance in this award-winning film. Or would Picasso have found this tale about a humble gardener sentimental?

For Picasso *Limelight* also had meaning in terms of the physical changes time had wrought in Chaplin and how these had modified the entire nature of his art.

"The real tragedy," Picasso said, "lies in the fact that Chaplin can no longer assume the physical appearance of the clown because he's no longer slender, no longer young, and no longer has the face and expression of his 'little man' but that of a man who's grown old. His body isn't really him anymore. Time has conquered him and turned him into another person. And now he's a lost soul—just another actor in search of his individuality and he won't be able to make anybody laugh."

I wondered how Picasso would have viewed Peter Sellers's own battle with aging? In 1976 when Peter and I were together I saw that he could still make his private and public audiences laugh. Nevertheless, Blake Edwards had wanted Peter to have a facelift to continue his Pink Panther films. Peter was upset over this. Had the aging process diminished Peter Sellers's ability to express himself comically so that he no longer could appear to be funny? Did he just look like an old man trying to be funny? Peter's box office success, however, disproved that the aging process was damaging his star power. In 1976, I thought Peter looked great, but it seems that Peter fell under the influence of Blake and his own self-doubt, and did have a facelift, which is apparent in *Being There*.

What disturbed Picasso most about *Limelight*, as Françoise Gilot relates in *Life with Picasso*, was that it told the story of an aging clown who is ready to sacrifice himself and turn the young woman he loves over to a younger man and thus allow her to embark on her life as a woman. "That kind of altruism is ridiculous," Picasso said. "Just hand-me-down, threadbare romanticism. That's not my way of doing things. To claim that when you love somebody, you can accept the idea of seeing her go off with some young fellow is very unconvincing. I'd rather see a woman die, any day, than see her happy with someone else. I prefer to be honest and sincere and admit that I want to hold onto the person I love and not for anything in the world let her go."

Here Claude Picasso disagreed with his father's thinking. Claude let me go to Hollywood alone and face a whole roll call of men who wanted to experience me because I had tested for *The Fan Club* and was a *cause célèbre*, a new piece of human flesh, meat, thrown on the Hollywood canvas. Yet Claude would still tell me he loved me. But maybe the real truth was that Claude never loved me at all.

When Claude and I had been living in Paris, we went to see Peter Sellers in a Pink Panther film shown on the Champs Elysees. "He's so talented," Claude said about Peter. "He should do more of these films. A series. No one can play Inspector Clouseau like him."

I was a bit suspicious of Claude's sense of humor. While he admired Peter Sellers, he loved Jerry Lewis. As far as I was concerned the French had a limited understanding of wit. Jerry Lewis's humor was slapstick and was, I felt, passé. The English, who in my opinion ruled in the world of comedy, rarely laughed at Jerry Lewis. None of the Englishmen I knew worshipped Jerry Lewis whereas the French would line up in droves for his films. Years after they had been produced. Grandmère and Françoise and even Paloma would talk about JER-ry LEW-is like he was some sort of god.

I was convinced Claude liked Peter Sellers because of the slapstick quality in the Pink Panther films. Myself, I never liked this series. These films did not use Peter's subtlety in portraying characters authentically. The laughs that came from the situation and the character showed Peter's true talent, as in *The Lady*

Killers and *I'm All Right, Jack*. Not the slapstick, bumbling antics as in the Pink Panther films, which relied heavily on sight gags. Picasso might very well have liked them, however, since he was into visual comedy.

I understood Peter's aversion to filming more Pink Panther films. After the first few, Peter resented being identified with Inspector Clouseau and lost no love over Panther director Blake Edwards.

One night we were invited to dinner *chez* Edwards.

"*The Return of the Pink Panther* will be my last one," Peter said, driving us in his tiny Mercedes convertible to the Malibu home of Blake Edwards and Julie Andrews. "I think these Pink Panther scripts are getting worse."

"Why do you do them?"

"I tell them, NO! Then they come back with these astounding salaries and I can't refuse. Tonight he's trying to get me to do another one. I can't get enthusiastic about it. I know he needs me for the series, but I feel guilty when I accept and realize I'm getting typecast. This will be my last one! Then Blake keeps after me to have a facelift. I don't want one! What do you think?"

"Peter, you don't need one. Tell him absolutely no!"

"Maybe he's right." I could tell Peter was thinking, "I'm an ugly-looking comic. Maybe a facelift will make me feel better about myself?"

I had wondered if Picasso had been right about Charlie Chaplin and how his aging had destroyed his comedy on film. Some part of me wondered if Peter did need a facelift. He already had had all his teeth capped and was always dyeing his hair for different parts.

"I don't look fondly at operations. I have a bad heart and surgery is difficult for me. But Blake keeps harping about my double chins and how bad I look with them on film."

"Peter, try to accept yourself. You're loved by so many people just as you are. Don't change a thing. Love yourself? Don't listen to Blake! Do you think we should turn around and have dinner at a Jack-in-the-Box?"

He laughed. "Well, that's kind of you, dear, to make me feel good about myself. Thanks. We'll see. I know I don't want a facelift. Yet."

When we arrived *chez* Edwards, we were greeted by two tightly smiling faces.

"Hello, Peter, darling," Julie said, kissing Peter on both his cheeks.

"Hello, my dear," Peter said and returned a cold smile. The ice and scalpel were in the air for the entire evening.

"And hello, Blake. This is Carole Mallory," Peter said, coolly to Blake.

"Peter and Carole, this is Burt and Dinah," Blake said as we all exchanged hellos and tried futilely to make small talk. Nothing helped. Burt Reynolds and Dinah Shore were sweet and genial, but Peter remained silent most of the night. Burt seemed intimidated by Peter and didn't tell many stories. We all sat and listened in silence while Peter and I drank too much.

"Julie, I'm sorry to have to go so soon, but I have this tremendous headache." Everyone knew Peter was fabricating his discomfort. He didn't care what they thought. Peter was getting back at Blake. He knew Blake needed him and wanted to make sure Blake made this the last Panther script. Above all Peter wanted Blake to think Peter was in control.

I was nervous around these people and more eager to leave than Peter. When we left, I was a bit tipsy, and so was he. He rarely showed it then.

After my first date with Peter Sellers, we returned to his old Spanish-style home, which I had left my toy poodle, Tutu, to guard. I seldom went anywhere without him. When Tutu was with me, I felt Claude wasn't far behind.

Peter's living room seemed to be half-filled with stereo equipment. "Would you like to hear some jazz or early Beatles records?" he asked.

"Oh, I love the Beatles." I said.

"I could have invested in them when they began. Instead I backed the film *The Magic Christian*. Suffered a great loss. Ah, but I do like its soundtrack. Nevertheless, it isn't quite worth two million."

"It's one of my favorite records. I have it at home. The film was great, Peter. Ahead of its time."

"We had a lot of fun doing it. But a two million loss somehow made it less funny. Would you like to see the rest of the house? I would like to show you the second floor. There's a bedroom that has a comfortable king-sized mattress and there's ample room for two. It is a recession and we shouldn't allow space to be wasted."

"Umm, I hate to waste space, myself, but do you think the bed could hold three? Tutu sleeps with me every night. An actress needs a watchdog in Hollywood."

"I'm sure we can arrange accommodations to suit his needs. Oui, Monsieur Tutu?" Peter smiled. He spoke perfect French to my best friend. Peter loved animals and was always kind to Tutu.

After listening to the soundtrack to *A Hard Day's Night*, we retired to Peter's masculine-looking bedroom, decorated in heavy, somber tones with wooden beams overhead. The maid had prepared his bed, pulling down the dark brown sheets. Stereo equipment was all around, as it had been downstairs. Peter loved gadgets—anything electrical—but, as I would discover, he never knew how to make these appliances work properly. (Like my father and me, as it happened.)

In his bathroom Peter had electric toothbrushes, a shoe-polishing machine, a portable cassette player, and a mini-stereo transistor radio. He loved music and never went anywhere without it.

Peter had an adjoining bathroom whose walls were covered by mirrors. Here I prepared myself for bed while Tutu watched, uttering an occasional growl. Pulling a terrycloth robe over my lace bikini panties, I locked Tutu in the *salle de bain* and walked out while opening my robe, pretending I was modeling the emperor's new clothes.

"My, you have a lovely body," Peter said in a whisper.

"Thank you, Mr. P. All the better to please you with."

"Come, let me look at you. That robe doesn't suit you."

I dropped the robe and sat on top of him.
"Did you bring the wine up, Peter? I'm thirsty."
"Yes, my dear, of course."
He held me and we kissed.
"What beautiful breasts you have. Let me look at them."
"Kiss them, Peter. The left one first. She's jealous. The right one seems to get all the attention."

I kissed him all over his hairy body. He had hair everywhere. He even had it on his back. I liked it. He reminded me of a giant panda bear. I would learn that he didn't like his hair and felt ashamed of it.

"I want to be inside you. Oh, Carole, you feel so wonderful. Oh!" he said, moaning, and he came.

I didn't. I hadn't gotten started. Oh, well. Time. We needed time. Anyway, I was too drunk to feel anything myself.

"Oh, Carole, Carole, Carole, what you do to me! I feel so good with you. So sexual. I want to make love to you all night," he said, sipping his wine.

Tutu was scratching at the bathroom door.
"Can I let Tutu out, Peter? He eats shoes when I'm making love."
"But of course. Whatever your little heart desires, my dear."

Tutu squealed as I opened the door. I held him and kissed him, too. Then he jumped on the bed with Peter and me.

"I love to make love. Tomorrow will be better. Before my heart attack, I could go for hours."

"What happened to you, Peter?"

"I've always had a bad heart. My father died of a heart attack. And the doctors warned me about my condition." He saddened dramatically. "When I first met Britt Ekland we had an active sex life. She was told by the doctors about my weak heart. Still one night she shoved amyl nitrate under my nose without warning me. I had seven heart attacks in a row. I've never been able to forgive her for it. I'm not the lover I was then, but I feel I can be with you."

"Oh, Peter, we drank too much. How are we going to feel in the morning?"

"Darling, I couldn't feel any better than when I'm holding you," he said, popping a red sleeping pill and within seconds was asleep. After I heard Peter and Tutu snore in unison, I grabbed the bottle of Valium that I carried with me and washed one down with white wine—like I usually did. I remembered Jonas Salk telling me in Paris that this was dangerous and could put me in a coma. What did he know? my ego said to myself. He invented the polio vaccine. What did that have to do with Valium? Wide-eyed, I looked around the dark and gloomy room. Everyone was at rest but me. Deep inside, I felt sad and alone. What was I doing with my life? Why wasn't I happy? I missed Claude—that was why. I wondered if he was having sex with someone to forget about me. I was hoping Peter would help me to forget Claude. But this didn't seem to be happening.

When we awakened, I thought I'd try again to have sex with Peter. First I sneaked out of bed and brushed my teeth.

"Bonjour, Monsieur Sel-laires," I said in my finest French.

Peter turned away from me.

I imagined he wanted to sleep more. I didn't.

"Peter, rise and shine. *C'est l'heure*! I want y-o-u for breakfast." I sang off key.

"I'm hungry."

He pulled the sheet over him and pushed my hands away, pulling my body against his. He held me. "I don't feel like it now, my darling. Don't be angry. We need time, remember?"

I was confused. Hurt. Again I felt alone. What was I doing wrong? Maybe it was me.

With Claude there had never been this problem. Claude liked me to open the boutique morning, noon, and night. But Peter wasn't Claude. Thinking about Claude only made me feel worse. Where was he? I wondered as I grabbed the bottle of leftover wine.

One morning I realized Peter was unable to have an erection sober. I think maybe he was too filled with self-loathing. Alcohol temporarily masked that and freed him from his demonic thoughts about himself.

Laughter also relaxed him, and took his mind off his deep feelings of inadequacy. I myself never thought that Peter was inadequate. I thought that he felt inadequate.

Over the months, as we pranked, mucked about, and drank, I was to realize how superstitious, even paranoid Peter could be. Always the saving grace was his sense of humor. Laughing was what Peter did best and what he enjoyed doing the most, especially with his friends, all of whom could match him gag for gag. And laughter was what I needed to forget Claude. For me Peter was like a doctor's prescribed painkiller. One day I would need a refill, however—which proved unobtainable.

Peter was happiest trying to be a bad little boy. His form of a supreme compliment to one of his mates was to play a practical joke on them or to "take the piss out of them," as the English would call it.

I remember one special game, invented by Stanley Kubrick, who was a father figure in mischief to Peter and to his pals. This game remains to this day one of Hollywood's best-kept secret pranks.

On this particular night, a roomful of people, including director John Schlesinger of *Darling* and *Midnight Cowboy*, sat by in hysterics or, like Peter, rolled around on the floor out of control, as the town's most gullible and glamorous stars were taken for a ride. The game entailed one guest making up a wildly peculiar voice and character; then gathering personal tidbits about certain celebrities from everybody in the room; then securing the celebrities' phone numbers and calling them as the fantasy character. Since the caller was equipped with intimate facts about the person called, the star-victim could be strung along into thinking the made-up caller was someone they'd been introduced to, but didn't recollect. Once convinced of the authenticity of the fictitious acquaintance the star could be convinced to hold long, nonsensical conversations, since they were afraid of offending someone who might be important. As a result, many nonexistent nobodies got invited to a lot of A-list parties. They never showed, of course, but the hosts never wondered why. So the game continued, with those fooled Raquel Welch,

Debbie Reynolds, Doris Day and Elizabeth Taylor (although they never suspected it). Only Bette Davis didn't fall for it. She hung up.

Another game Peter loved playing was with his stereo and its equipment. It was our X-rated version of hide and seek. He carried a wireless microphone in and out of every room as well as the closet. Dr. Strangelove's and Inspector Clouseau's voices were heard throughout the house challenging me to find them. Then it was my turn to hide when I heard, "Comminsie here mine liebshin. I vantzu rub catsup und mayonnaise in your NOOKS UND CRANNIES. I'M COMIN ZU GET YOU...!

Like Grandmère's kitchen in Paris, Peter's kitchen was filled with fresh vegetables. Every day the housekeeper went shopping for food. "In England, you see, we are civilized," Peter would say. "Every good Englishman has a garden and grows his own fresh veggies. We don't go around eating all this frozen, jumbo-sized, economy-sized, or deep-fried junk you Americans subscribe to. How can you dare eat this frozen nonsense! Why it's like eating death. Furthermore, there's no flavor. It's all artificial color. It all turns my stomach, I'm afraid."

"Peter, we have health food shops where everything is fresh."

"They are few and expensive. In England every grocery store is health food. We wouldn't dream of buying the frozen way of life you Americans do. Let alone eating it! Then you have the homogenized, pasteurized, sterilized and sanitized lot. My dear, labels, labels, labels. It's amazing Americans don't get them all bollixed up! Could I please have a sanitized open-faced milkshake with a pasteurized straw?"

In France every store was a health food store, too. In Paris, but especially in the countryside. In the south of France, the women carried beautiful hand-woven baskets that they would take shopping and pile in all sorts of herbs and fresh vegetables. Artists, Picasso among them, often drew and painted these women carrying their produce as it was a splendid sight. In America we used the shopping cart, which may have been practical, but would have been an eyesore to the likes of Picasso. I loved the fresh vegetables in Paris that were sold by vendors at intersections as well as in mini-markets like Felix Potin. And like the English, Grandmère had her own garden in back of the carriage house. That was where Claude and I were going to have our wedding. Well, maybe one day, I told myself.

All of Peter's friends had great senses of humor. It didn't matter who they were or what they did, as long as Peter could laugh with them.

One night Keith Moon of the *Who* escorted Peter and me to a party at Hugh Hefner's Playboy mansion.

"Got a surprise ferya, matey," Keith said, standing by the door grinning gold tooth to tooth. "Come on out 'ere an' look what I got fer us 'specially for the night'! We got to go to Hef's Den of Iniquity in style, mate, right?"

Peter looked out the door. "Well, bollix me, boy!"

There was a gold, stretch Cadillac limousine with its driver, a woman jockey—cap and all—posing regally while holding open a door.

"Eh, matey, pretty swell for the nitie night at Hef's, wouldn't ya say?"

Everyone laughed except for our chauffeurette, who remained frozen in her prepaid pose.

By the time we arrived at the mansion we had downed a quart of vodka. Hefner's electronic bodyguard approved our entrance. Women were welcome, but men who were not celebrities or personal friends of Hefner were not. We drove up the circular driveway passing peacocks strolling on the lawn.

"That's some bird, eh, mate?" Keith said. "Like to take 'er home?" Keith laughed, flashing his gold teeth. "Let's hit the main joint, shall we?"

"Pleased to be your guest, Mr. Moon," Peter said. "Let's not hang around if this is one of those crowded affairs. I'm not really in the mood for an excessive amount of bunnies."

We walked into the mansion, which was like a big fraternity house. An enormous bodyguard stood by the huge wooden door. The foyer was tiny and the staircase to the bedrooms was on the left just past the entrance. It seemed the bodyguard was watching the front door as well as the bedrooms. The first room we walked into reminded me of a ballroom. The walls were light brown wood and the carpet was hunter green. Fresh flowers were on every end table.

Then we entered the dining room and surveyed the gigantic buffet. There was a queue of guests and bunnies, and it reminded me of an elegant cafeteria. Silver bainsmarie were used to keep the food warm. Dinner was available all night for 300 guests.

Peter sat quietly in a corner. "Darling, I don't think I can take too much more. I feel a bit walled in—if you know what I mean."

"Whatever you want, Peter," I said, lying, as I wanted to stay and check out the clandestine action. I was more interested in the bunnies' behavior than Peter was. They seemed like nice girls who wore little. There was a Kansas City freshness to most of them, and with a budding journalist's curiosity I wanted to know how the sex life of the mansion functioned. I never did find out. I watched the staircase to the bedrooms and the bodyguard who I was told remained all night. There was no action there. Having an affair with a bunny was not as simple as people thought.

"Let's get out of 'ere, mate," Keith said to Peter. Keith wasn't interested in the bunnies either. "Let's check out tha game room. It's across the lawn."

We walked past the bodyguard, beyond the big wooden door and across the sprawling lawn. It was a vision straight out of Alice in Wonderland, as we passed peacocks in the moonlight and came upon a small cottage.

"This is it, folks. Choose your game. Moon's me name," Keith said, laughing before he attacked a pinball machine, one of thirty. Lights were flashing and buzzers were going off while Peter found a seat in the corner by a player piano.

"I'm not much for these games, I'm afraid, Carole, but you play if you like. I'll watch," Peter said.

I played one game of Electric Space Bunny and then a game of pool with Keith. Peter joined us. A bevy of bunnies had followed us from the mansion and were asking Keith and Peter to sing on the player piano.

Keith gave us one song. He sat in courtly fashion at the upright and pretended enthusiastically to be playing while we all joined a chorus of "Bye Bye Blackbird." Peter laughed and sang along. He and Keith seemed more interested in each other's jokes and performances than the surroundings. Soon Peter tired of the whole thing.

"Shall we go back to San Ysidro and listen to some music," Peter said, sighing. "I'm rather tired of all this."

"Whatever your fancy laces desire, Matey mate," Keith said. And we went back to Peter's home and listened to more *Goon Show* recordings, Peter's favorite entertainment.

A year later Keith Moon would die from a drug overdose.

I wondered how Claude would have behaved at the Playboy mansion. Did the French have an equivalent? After all there was the Marquis de Sade. But that was literature. Then again there was Madame Claude, the famous French madam, but I never knew of Claude going to brothels or of being attracted to call girls. Claude rarely made me jealous of other women. He never read *Playboy* or *Penthouse*, though when we met, he did assist a friend who was making porno films. Still I never saw this side of him. Oh, he did have an obsession with flat-chested red heads. The exhibit of his photographs at which we had first met showed shots of a naked redhead and a big stuffed bird. No one could figure out this fantasy, but voyeurism never presented a problem in our relationship.

The closest I would come to feeling jealous of other women was when Paloma would invite Claude to fashion shows. Here, he was attracted to other women. Claude was turned on by elegance and style, not pictures of *Playboy* bunnies or Hollywood's plastic beauty.

Peter Sellers was turned on by laughter and by the craft of acting. He was fond of Alec Guinness, who was in town filming *Murder by Death* with Peter. Alec was playing the role of the butler. One sunny day we lunched at the Inn of the Four Oaks in Beverly Glen. Alec Guinness was frail and thin, and his skin had a grey tone to it. He was terribly witty with a wonderful reserve. We drank mimosas, champagne and orange juice, until we were pissed. They shot back and forth all kinds of characters with funny accents until I felt as though I was at a Friars roast for their old films.

Picasso's Ghost

Then Peter talked about *Murder by Death* and Truman Capote, who was a member of the cast. "What are we to do with Truman? He's ruining our timing and we could have a flop if he continues to perform badly. Who cast him? Why?"

Alec Guinness looked with sympathy into Peter's eyes.

"With all the good actors, why Truman?" Peter said. "He's not one of us. His timing is atrocious. I've talked to David [cast member Niven) about this and he agrees. Should we talk to Ray [producer Stark), or do you think we could help the old boy to move a bit more quickly with his cues. He keeps missing them and it's bogging down the timing of the whole film!"

Alec Guinness nodded in agreement.

"I am so annoyed about this," Peter said. "I don't know what to do!"

"Well, Peter, we might be able to help Truman out, but you know it's really out of our hands," Alec Guinness said. "I'm afraid we just have to do the best we can. I'll have a talk with Truman if you think that would help."

I began to feel the need to defend Peter against accusations of being difficult to work with.

I remembered doing this with Claude and defending his photography with editors at magazines after Avedon had fired him.

Maybe Peter was difficult not because of his arrogance, but because he was a professional and a perfectionist. It seemed to me he wanted the best for everyone, and lacked patience with others with lesser talent.

I apparently did such a good job of trying to uphold Peter and his reputation that his publicist actually thanked me for taking care of him. What a nerve! Now, looking back, I realize this publicist, David Steinberg, was being kind. I simply didn't know how sick Peter was.

Peter never revealed his feelings to the outside world because, I felt, he was too filled with fear: fear of what people thought of him, fear of being ugly, fear of sudden death due to his weak heart, fear of starring in a flop, fear of growing old, fear of impotency, fear of being found out to have these fears. I believed that we all possessed most of these fears in some form and they could endanger our lives if we were to allow them to take control of us. For me Peter was an object lesson in the truth that fame, talent, money, and success don't guarantee happiness.

Aggravated by the emotionally and physically ravaging effects of drinking and drug-taking, Peter turned his dislike for himself onto others, blaming and punishing those closest to him. He was misunderstood by so many—even by his family and even, at the time, by me.

I could tell that Peter hated his looks. He considered himself an ugly myopic in horrible glasses covered with disgusting long, black body hair. When he was depressed, he ate to excess, then developed a weight problem, which added to his self-loathing. With me he felt he was a sexual failure and was very, very lonely. I believed he drank and took drugs to feel less alone, but in time the alcohol and chemicals stopped working for him and joined the battle against himself.

The night of Peter's fatal heart attack four years later, he would drink a bottle of wine, smoke grass, and take a sleeping pill—his standard formula for getting to sleep. Given his damaged heart it's not surprising that this combination would finally prove lethal for him. I believe Peter was aware of the danger. I think he knew he was hurting himself, but he couldn't stop. Why should he? Nobody in Hollywood was making it easy for him. People were constantly offering him every drug in the world, including cocaine. You don't have to be a doctor to know how risky coke is for a man with his cardiac history, but that didn't stop his own doctor from pushing it on him. Why? Why didn't anybody care?

While we were together, I saw to it that Peter did not use cocaine, but we made up for it with drinking and marijuana. When the hangovers were too painful, we'd go on special diets. His favorite was steak and oranges. (Tutu ate steak *chez* Sellers.) This regime would be observed for a few days, then we'd celebrate conquering our willpower with a good bottle of wine and were back to begin again as the fun-loving drinkers we imagined we were.

When Peter was hung over, he could be nasty, and so could I, but normally he was a kind and great-hearted man, not only lavishing me with presents, but also honoring me with respect. This respect was refreshing for me after the disrespect I felt at the hands of Claude.

One morning on Peter's kitchen table, I noticed a script called *Being There*.

"What's this?" I asked.

"That, my dear, is a script I want to do very much. Do you know the writer, Jerzy Kosinski?"

"Yes."

"He's a wonderful writer and great friend. I believe in the project and want to make sure nothing goes wrong with the making of this film."

"What's it about?"

"A simple man who's a gardener. It's quite a moving story. Hal Ashby is going to direct. It's funny at the same time as it makes a serious statement. I'm so tired of these bloody Pink Panther films. I know *Being There* will be my finest film. I have this feeling about it. It's a short book. I'd appreciate your taking the time to read it."

Peter died not long after the film had its success. *Being There* was his goodbye kiss to us all.

While I was seeing Peter, I was studying improvisational comedy, and he couldn't have been more generous about helping me with my work.

"You must memorize as much as you can. That way you are free to create. I memorize the sound and rhythm I select. First I experiment with all the possibilities. Once I make a choice, I set it, and memorize it exactly. The gestures, sound and emphasis you make with the words are very important in comedy. I never leave anything to spontaneity. There is enough of that that happens naturally. You must take responsibility for your character. An actor is only as good as his or her choices."

The kitchen was Peter's favorite room to rehearse and to hang out. It was sunny with lots of blue and white Spanish tiles and modern chrome appliances. We could see the pool and the beautiful garden from this bright and cheery room. The rest of the house was dark and gloomy. We sat at the kitchen table —a butcher block—and had our meals. I often thought of Grandmère's kitchen and how the Picasso family gathered there as well. Peter's kitchen brought up thoughts of Claude. Would he be jealous of Peter's feelings for me?

Peter's secretary, and chauffeur, Burt Mortimer, who was also a friend, was often with us in the kitchen. One day Burt came in laughing with a clipping from Nigel Dempster's gossip column in the London *Daily Mail*, which published a photo of Claude and me and a separate one of Peter Sellers under the headline "YOUNG PICASSO'S GIRL CAROLE FINDS A FRIEND IN SELLERS." It began, "Peter Sellers, 49, has propelled himself into yet another outburst of love during his California sojourn. Carole Mallory has become the sole object of his overwhelming affections. They have become inseparable. Carole's most recent boy friend was Claude Picasso, 27, the illegitimate son of the legendary artist. The French courts granted him 5 million pounds from Pablo's fortune last year." Under Seller's photo was his quote about me, "Really divine."

Picasso's Ghost

Young Picasso's girl Carole finds a friend in Sellers

THE overworked libido of Peter Sellers, 49, has propelled him into yet another burst of love during his Californian sojourn in the romantic ambience of Bev Hill.

After meeting the exotic beside the swimming pool of the posh Bel-Air, New York fashion model Carole Mallory became the object of his overwhelming affections.

They have become inseparable and Sellers paid court only a week ago, it revealed, to Susan George and Liza Farringer and declared: 'She is a really divine girl.'

Brunette Carole, who is attempting to establish a Hollywood career and has been rewarded by a fleeting role in *Funny Lady* has not been short of famous escorts.

Her most recent boy friend was Claude Picasso, 27, the illegitimate son of the legendary artist. The French courts granted him £5 million from Pablo's fortune last year.

Carole has also been a close companion of producer Sy Litvinoff of *A Clockwork...*

Sellers: 'Really divine'

Daily Mail clipping

Peter read the article giggling. He liked publicity, courted a good relationship with the press, and seemed pleased to see our names linked. I wondered what Claude would think about this article. I still loved Claude. Peter had been a way of forgetting him. Well, trying to.

The end of my romance with Peter, when it came, would come over something which initially seemed irritating, but unimportant—one of Peter's less amusing hobbies, photography.

Peter was proud of my modeling portfolio and wanted to take a photo of me for it. He had seen Claude's photos in my portfolio and had wanted to have his there, too.

"Peter, I don't really like to be photographed. My features are pretty uneven and I'm afraid I'll disappoint you. It's not easy to take a good portrait of me."

He kept hounding me. Finally I agreed. Peter and I were emotionally alike—nervous wrecks. For the session I brought along Tutu. Maybe he'd save the day. He did. The Polaroids of Tutu and me were beautiful. I was glad it was over.

When Peter picked the film up from the lab, he was ecstatic. "Carole, you must come over right away and look at these. They're marvelous!"

"Peter, I can't. I'm filming *Fantasy Island*. Remember?"

The following day, he edited them and called again. "They're O.K, Carole, but not as good as I had expected. We'll have to do a re-shoot. Can you come over and go through the slides with me? I must have your opinion."

"Peter, I'm still filming that *Fantasy Island* episode. Tomorrow I'm through. I'll be over then. Don't worry." I was really trying to comfort myself. Now I was upset. I felt I had let Peter down exactly as I had feared I would do.

By the third day, Peter was depressed. "Could you please come by, Carole, and pick up your photos? I'm not pleased with them and don't want them around the house. I'm sorry the session was such a failure," he said, harshly.

Before I went to Peter's, I made a date for dinner that evening. I was afraid Peter had rejected me. I was sure he didn't want to see me again, so I thought I'd protect my hurt feelings and reject him first. I didn't feel I was rich, famous, or pretty enough for him. I allowed this photo session to confirm these negative thoughts. What was really happening was that our mutual low self-images had declared war.

When I walked into the kitchen, Peter looked gloomy and despondent. He showed me the pictures slowly. At this point, I was furious and unable to have an opinion about anything.

"Would you have dinner with me this evening?" he asked.

I was thrown. I had thought he was through with me. What was I to do?

I didn't know how to tell Peter what I was feeling. I couldn't talk about my feelings. I couldn't tell Peter I still cared for him. Besides, I really missed Claude. My love for Claude had haunted my relationship with Peter.

"I'm sorry, Peter, but I already have a date," I said, stammering. I knew after this moment I had ended our affair. Peter's ego couldn't take rejection—and neither could mine. I had felt that I was inadequate and not pretty enough, and Peter felt he was inadequate as a photographer and his photos not good enough.

After dating for almost a year, we broke up over trivial matters. Sad.

I still have Peter's portrait today, and it is as beautiful as it always was and is on the cover of this book.

Peter Sellers photo of me

My photo of Peter Sellers

Death and Dissolution

In late winter of 1976, my father died. Devastated, I left Tutu with a neighbor and flew from Hollywood to Valley Forge, Pennsylvania. For my wedding to Claude I had bought my father a beautiful navy blue wedding suit, which, as it turned out, he wore once—in his coffin. I only saw his arm jutting out from the open coffin. My mother was kissing him and wanted me to, but I would not look at him. "Oh, Carole, you're being so silly. He looks so peaceful. He's at rest now and not twitching anymore from that Parkinson's."

"No, Mother. I want to remember him as he was."

"They did such a good job on him. Come on, why don't you give him a kiss? He loved you so. It will be the last time you ever see your father, and you'll always regret not kissing him."

My mother had been taking my father's medication. So had my sister. I had as well.

We were all taking Valium, Phenobarbital, and whatever, but Valium was the family drug of choice. I had taken a pill before the funeral. It helped me with my shaking from fear, like it helped my father with his. I never did look at my father in his coffin. But I can still see that left arm jutting out of the coffin, covered in a brand new, navy blue suit sleeve with a clean, super-white cuff. And his fingers, thin and long like mine, pointing upward, as if they were holding up the coffin lid, inviting me in. My father was special and should never have been buried like anyone else…ever.

My yellow dress was covered in tears. I cried driving along the turnpike on the way home to New York. I wanted to die. As I was driving out of the Lincoln Tunnel, I looked up to see a gigantic billboard with a photo of my face smiling under a yellow umbrella while I sipped Gordon's Gin. I looked so happy in the photo. It was bigger than life.

I saw that I once had been happy and successful like my father had always wanted me to be. Could I do that again? I was going to make up for my father's suffering. Show these people who hurt him. Never let people hurt me as they had hurt him. Nobody was going to give me a lobotomy. Not my mother, my sister, Claude, or Hollywood.

And when I drove out of the Lincoln Tunnel on my way out of New York, and again took notice of the huge billboard of my smiling face under that yellow umbrella sipping gin with a man I didn't even know, I thought I could get myself together. Gordon's Gin had helped me then and could help me today.

Gordon's Gin. That's what I needed. Where was a bar?

The next morning, hung over, I returned to Hollywood.

Claude called not long after my affair with Peter Sellers had been announced in London's *Daily Mail*.

"That was quite an announcement you two had in the London paper. When are you both making it permanent?" Claude asked, bitterly.

"Oh, Claude, we're just friends. How did you hear about the article?"

"A friend of mine brought it over to the apartment."

"My father died, Claude."

"Sorry to hear that. I liked him."

"Wish you could have been here for his funeral." I paused. "Some friends you have."

"He was a friend. I don't talk to him anymore."

"When am I going to see you?"

"I'm still dealing with the estate. When I get further along, I'll call you."

"Can we meet in our NY apartment for a rendezvous?" I asked hesitantly.

"I'll have to get back to you about that."

I was happy to hear Claude's Spanish jealousy and was even happier to hear that he still cared. But I was happiest that Peter Sellers had been there to help me laugh just before my father died.

I hated that Claude dodged seeing me, however. I felt ignored and dismissed. My dreams of his coming to Hollywood to rescue me turned into nightmares.

In the spring of 1976, my New York modeling agent called to tell me I had been booked by a major French client. I returned to New York for a week and was photographed by Bill King for a French underwear campaign. I was to be pulling the shirt off a male model to get a peek at what he was wearing underneath. The campaign was called, *"Les discrets de Jil."* Billboards on the Champs Élysées and all over Paris proclaimed, *"Voilà des Jil au couleurs des chemises."*

One day Claude called. "Well, Chérie, you are all over Paris."

"How's that?"

"There are posters of you everywhere. I think you're haunting me." Claude laughed.

I didn't.

"Is this why you called?" I asked.

"Partially. The rent is due on the Sovereign and I wondered if you were going to pay half of it."

I couldn't believe it. Or rather I could believe it. Miser Claude—just like his father. "I don't have it, Claude. The lease is in both our names. Why can't you pay for it with all that money you have from the estate?"

"Chérie, it hasn't come through yet."

"So ask your mother or grandmother. I'm not backing you anymore, Claude."

"It's not about backing me. It's about taking responsibility for your obligation."

"Your obligation was to marry me. When are you going to do that?"

"Let's not go there."

"Sorry, Claude, you'll have to take care of the rent with your six million. I think you can afford it."

"Sorry you feel that way," Claude said.

"Ditto." I said.

"By the way, we are going to have to move the furniture out of the Sovereign in the not too distant future."

"So this is why you called?" I reached for a bottle of wine.

"One of the reasons. Are you making arrangements?"

I opened the wine.

"Not yet. Claude, I have to go. Someone's at the door," I said, lying through my tears.

We hung up. I drank the bottle of wine, took a Valium, and passed out.

Later that week I got the following letter from Claude.

"I have tried to think out this problem. It's hard," Claude wrote. "I can go on paying for the Sovereign although that straps me down a lot since I don't use it. Now if you want to stay in it, I would like to work something out with you ...either we go half on it paying half the rent. You staying in it until the lease runs out which I think is next year or else you try to find another place and I try to get rid of this place since I don't need it."

I had trouble believing that Claude had forgotten what I had done for him. He still wanted me to pay half the rent when he was now suddenly a millionaire after all the years I had supported him. Was there any chance of our getting married? I was still hoping that Claude needed time to adjust to his new wealth and new position as administrator of Picasso's estate.

Goodbar Role

In 1976 when *Looking for Mr. Goodbar* was being cast, I was being considered for one of the leading roles.

This film starred Diane Keaton and traced the sexual awakening of a young schoolteacher searching for excitement outside her mundane existence. Originally in search of the perfect man, she begins to frequent singles bar; she begins losing control of her life as her sexual appetite grows. Quiet and reserved by day, sexually voracious bar hopper at night, she begins to dabble in drugs and unstable men. Her self-destructive behavior is a means of escaping her numbing existence and testing her boundaries, providing excitement in an otherwise safe and boring life. One of her sexual partners, played by Richard Gere, turns jealous, possessive, and violent. Ultimately her sexual addiction and high-risk behavior put her life in danger, and she picks up someone truly dangerous in a bar. She is murdered.

Having been a schoolteacher, a blossoming alcoholic, and curious enough about sex to call up Warren Beatty to ask him to be with me, I was perfect for this part, but I was not a star and alas, Diane Keaton was cast instead of me. But Freddie Fields, the producer, thought I was right for the role of Diane's alcoholic sister. Fields, who cofounded the agency CMA and who represented Spielberg, Newman, Redford, and McQueen at one time, has been called the most powerful agent in Hollywood. It has been written that he was instrumental in the careers of Marilyn Monroe, Woody Allen, and Peter Sellers.

By 1976, Freddie Fields was no longer an agent but a producer. He called my agent and brought me into Paramount Studios to meet the award-winning director Richard Brooks. Brooks directed *In Cold Blood*, which was nominated for an Oscar, as well as *Blackboard Jungle* and *Cat on a Hot Tin Roof*. He won an Oscar for his screenplay of *Elmer Gantry*.

Nervous while being eyed by these two powerful men, I stood in my white khakis and red silk shirt as I listened to Richard Brooks. "We've tried to get your *Fan Club* test from Columbia, but the producers, Larry Gordon and Peter Guber, say that it is lost at Beacon's storage."

A few weeks later, Tuesday Weld was cast in the role for which I was being considered, but I was chosen for another part, the role of Marvella. She was a friend of the Tuesday Weld character who does drugs all night with two men and invites Diane into an orgy. While I had never been in an orgy or wanted to be in an orgy, I was an actress, and this was supposedly a coveted part in a prestigious film.

It was a week's work with a lengthy scene with Tuesday and Diane, as well as the orgy scene.

I was eager to meet and to work with Diane Keaton, whose image was one of warmth and humor. I was apprehensive about working with Tuesday Weld, whose image was of the bad girl, the spoiled, difficult beauty. Hollywood images are often the fabrication of publicists and studios and far from the truth. Tuesday was the warm generous actress to work with, while Diane was cold and withholding. I realized Diane was guarded because she was working on the inner life of her character and did not want anyone to disturb her creative process. Still, Tuesday could have felt the same way, but she extended herself to me in an act of friendship.

During filming director Brooks sternly said, "Now after your line, I want a big laugh from you, Carole."

Tuesday could tell I was nervous. Laughter on cue is one of the most difficult feats for an actor. This actor, anyway. "Some direction he gave you," Tuesday said with a smirk. "Most directors don't know how to direct. I'll help you. Start the scene. I'll give you something."

Brooks shouted, "Action."

I recited my line, "Sounds like a butch nun."

As Tuesday started to walk behind the sofa she tripped, which caused me to let out the big laugh that Brooks had wanted from me.

Brooks said, "Good take, Carole."

Tuesday Weld had directed the scene, not Richard Brooks. She had helped a terrified me.

Diane did not offer advice or support for me. She was afraid of Richard Brooks as well. Every member of the cast in this scene was fearful of Richard Brooks, who did more screaming than speaking—except Tuesday Weld, who was fearless.

The orgy was another closed set after the party scene.

It begins with Tuesday, two men, and me passed out in the bedroom. As Diane opens the door, I gesture with my cigarette, inviting her into the orgy. Stunned to see four naked motionless bodies in her sister's bedroom, Diane rejects my offer and closes the door.

Filming an orgy was long, hard work. Boring. All four actors were face down on the bed and could not move. The men's genitalia, though not to be seen on camera, were covered with black tape. Tuesday wore nude-colored pantyhose. She wrapped a black bra around her waist to hide the top of her stockings. Wardrobe had not given me this option. I was closest to the camera and this wardrobe trick would not have worked for me, or so I was told. It took eight hours of lying motionless on a bed to film, which had the actors' bodies almost paralyzed. No one was permitted to talk. I was propped on my elbows signaling Diane to come into the orgy. My breasts were not visible. It was a long shot of four bodies in the bedroom. A close-up of my face, then Diane's reaction.

Because my body was rigid from not being able to move, when a break was called for lunch, I had difficulty getting up from the bed. Brooks saw me struggling and offered to give me a massage off camera.

A table covered by a plastic mat was in the corner of the dark set. Director Brooks massaged my shoulders as I lay face down on the mat. A cloth covered the bottom of my body. Crew members were off to one side. I was uncomfortable with the authoritative Brooks. Since he was my director and I was in awe of his Oscar-quality work, I was afraid to say no. Naïve, gullible fool that I was, I should not have allowed him to touch me.

In 1977, after the filming of *Goodbar*, Richard Brooks and Jean Simmons, whom he met while filming *Elmer Gantry*, divorced. I had met Jean Simmons in passing and she was a sober, charming, and beautiful lady. After she divorced Brooks, he became part of Hugh Hefner's family and part of the soft porn entrepreneur's feudal estate, where he was observed by satirist Clive James. "Hefner's estate teemed with voluptuous young women," James wrote, "and the dining room, where free hamburgers were available 24 hours a day, was impressively populated with Hollywood male notables. Sad to say, most of them were superannuated male lechers. The film director, Richard Brooks, was typical. He had been here chomping on free hamburgers while he eyed the women. He was in Hef's hamburger heaven, sizing up the poontang on his way to a final resting place in Hillside Memorial Park."

After the filming of *Goodbar*, Freddie Fields, who would later produce *American Gigolo*, invited me along with some other friends of his for lunch at his home in Malibu. I wanted to get some sun and to swim in the ocean. Living in West Hollywood, I was denied these luxuries. When I arrived at about noon, he offered me a drink and showed me where to change into my bikini. He had on a swimsuit. As I came out of the bathroom, he led me to a lounge chair on his deck overlooking the ocean. No other guests had arrived and perhaps were never coming. We sat side by side sunbathing. "Here, try some of this. Rub it between your legs. It feels good," Freddie Fields, one of Hollywood's first super agents said to me as he handed me a bottle of cocaine. I excused myself, put on my clothing, and drove home.

Richard Brooks and Freddie Fields's advances were emblematic of how the respected male power structure operated on young and nubile starlets. We were told to audition for a sexy part and dress in as revealing a way as possible, then to preen in front of male producers, who later would try to get their hands on our bodies.

In 1986 when Norman Mailer was casting his film *Tough Guys Don't Dance*, he wanted to audition Cathy Moriarty, a stunning actress who had just played Jake La Motta's wife in *Raging Bull*. "You know I really like Cathy Moriarty, but her husband had to come with her on the audition and that was rather insulting," Norman told me.

Cathy Moriarty's husband had the right idea. On auditions actresses needed bodyguards. The audition, or casting couch, was much like that of a customer choosing choice cattle for slaughter. In Hollywood these customers were called producers and directors. Starlets, often innocent women, were the cattle led to slaughter by these respected lecherous males who, because of their box office success, Oscar-worthy work, or reputations as super-agents who masterminded the careers of luminaries, enjoyed tremendous power. But who doesn't know this?

Mr. Goodbar

After filming *Goodbar*, I ran into Richard Gere on the Paramount lot. We laughed and hugged, and he invited me to lunch.

Richard, who in 1999 would be named by *People* magazine "one of the sexiest men alive," was beginning his metamorphosis. No longer the bad boy, he was jovial, positive, and a gentleman. The insecurity, leather jackets, and motorcycles of the late 60s had vanished.

He chose an unpretentious restaurant around the corner from the studio. It had red leather banquettes, shaded lamps, and a soft-spoken clientele. We slid into a booth.

"So here we are in Hollywood. Long way from acting class on West 56th Street above that Chinese laundry," Richard said.

"Remember those days? Brad Davis, Penny Milford," I said.

The waiter gave us menus.

"I still see Penny from time to time."

"How'd you meet?"

"We were in *Long Time Coming and a Long Time Gone*, a play in New York. She played Joan Baez."

"How long did you date?"

"We were together seven years."

"Are you still involved?"

"Do you mean are we having sex?" Richard said.

"No, that's none of my business."

"That's right," Richard smiled as we ordered. "How'd you get into acting?"

"Doing commercials. Spokesperson. English Leather. All My Men Wear English Leather or They Wear Nothing at All."

"That was you?" Richard laughed.

"What made you want to be an actor?"

"Even back in high school I liked writing music and doing plays," he said. "I played the guitar, bass, piano. One day I'd love to do a musical." (In 2002 Richard starred in *Chicago*.)

"I played the piano, too," I said. "For years. Hated the lessons.. Miss Dutton was my teacher."

"What a name! Miss Dutton. Sounds like a spinster. Did she rap your knuckles with a ruler when you hit a wrong key?"

"No, but she wore a hat and veil every time I had a lesson. Remember 'Moonlight Sonata?'"

"Beethoven! Sure do." Richard chuckled as he put his napkin on his lap.

"I was in the band and orchestra."

"What'd you play?"

"The clarinet and alto clarinet."

"The trumpet."

"I've let all that go," I said.

"Me, too. Except I think it helped me to get the understudy for Barry Botswick in *Grease*. Jump-started my career."

The waiter served our entrees.

"Where'd you go after high school?" I asked.

"Got a scholarship to Amherst in gymnastics of all things. Majored in psychology, dropped out after two years and got hired at the Provincetown Playhouse in about 69."

"Did plays at the Bucks County Playhouse in New Hope about that time. Madge in *Picnic*."

"I can see that," Richard said, sipping an iced tea. "So how's Tinsel Town treating you?"

"They sure hate New Yorkers."

"They pretend not to like us, but I'm not sure about that. Look, you and I are here. Diane and Tuesday are New Yorkers."

Picasso's Ghost

"Was there competition for your part?"

"Steven Keats was cast, but Freddie Fields wanted him to fix his teeth and scrape his face so he told Freddie to take a hike, and they cast me."

"Don't see you and Steven Keats as the same type."

"I don't either. I've starred in *Report to the Commissioner, Baby Blue Marine*, and *Strike Force*, and still I wasn't their first choice."

"Producers like to see us compete," I said. "Gives them power."

"It's sure great being in a film with you." Richard said, holding my hand on the table.

"Yeah, I miss our acting classes."

"I'll never forget that Blanche you did with Berry Berenson. You were great. All those nerve endings you weren't afraid to show."

"Fear."

"Pity we don't have any scenes together," Richard said, his eyes twinkling.

"How's Brooks?"

"A screamer. Furniture mover."

"Wyn taught us that, remember? How directors move furniture instead of performances."

"I remember more than that. Like that night we went back to your place." Richard's eyes glazed over.

"No. We didn't."

"You don't remember?" Richard said laughing. He removed his hand from mine.

"No, I don't."

"Carole, we made love."

"Richard, so much has gone down with Claude," I said, wondering if Richard was handing me a line. Because of my drinking, however, it was possible that we had had sex and I didn't remember.

"Yeah, what happened between you?"

"He keeps stalling about the wedding date," I said, sipping my bloody Mary.

"You mean it's still on?"

"He calls. We talk."

"His loss."

"We still have that apartment in New York."

"Look what you're doing with your life."

"I still have feelings for Claude."

"He was keeping you down. Probably jealous."

"He wanted to direct."

"That's it. Jealousy."

"Now I'm being directed by good directors," I said, putting dressing on my salad.

"What else have you done?"

"Peckinpah cast me in his last film, *Killer Elite*."

"That's great!" Richard said, biting into his cheeseburger.

"He was tough."

"Heard he was a tyrant on the set."

"Jimmy Caan and his entourage 'allegedly' turned Peckinpah onto cocaine during filming," I said, moving my fork around in my salad.

"Is that right?"

"One morning Sam offered me a B12 shot, amyl nitrate, alcohol, marijuana, or cocaine before a take. I chose the B12 shot."

"What was the scene?" Richard asked, looking depressed.

"In a bed with Jimmy Caan. I had a bikini bottom on and he kept holding me as Peckinpah yelled, 'Improvise.'"

"Bet that scene wasn't in the film."

"You got it. Peckinpah was so loaded by the end of filming that he stopped showing up. Directed through an assistant."

"The studio allowed that?"

"What could they do?"

"Send him to a rehab," Richard said under his breath.

"Sam wouldn't come out of his trailer. One day he OD'd on cocaine. Still was able to finish the film."

"How did *Killer Elite* do?"

"It was a flop." I signaled the waiter for a cup of coffee.

"I heard he dove one day into the Beverly Wilshire Hotel pool and there was no water in it," Richard said.

"That's right. Sam was drunk, yet lived."

"Amazing." Richard shook his head.

Picasso's Ghost

"His body tolerated so much abuse. Boy, he was paranoid. Must've been the coke."

"Bet he was hard to work with." Richard's concern for my feelings made me feel he cared about me.

"Impossible."

"This town is rough on women."

"How'd you deal with the 'Velvet Underground'?"

"What's that?" I had trouble believing Richard had not heard of it.

"The gay mafia that runs this town."

"They leave me alone," Richard said with a smile. "I think they know I'll blow their cover if they make advances."

"Surely they made passes toward you."

"Carole, no way."

"You're lucky."

"Got that right. You know my father wanted me to be a minister. You're talking to a Pilgrim."

"Get out of here!"

As we laughed our shoulders touched. I felt sparks. "My ancestors came over on the Mayflower."

"Really?"

" Really. I was raised strict Methodist."

"I was raised Lutheran and Pennsylvania Dutch."

"Your background and sexiness must make dirty old producers doubly hard for you."

"I survive, but after four years of acting classes with actors like you and Brad Davis and Penny, I end up with parts like I have in this film," I said without a smile.

"This is going to be a big film, Carole. It's important that you're in it. You'll be remembered."

"When I was in New York, I filmed *Stepford Wives*. I had a great part."

"You did. You were good."

"Come to Hollywood and parts get smaller."

"Give it time. Who directed *Stepford Wives*?"

"Bryan Forbes,'

"How was he?"

"Terrific. Caught me not listening in a scene and made me do it until it was right,"

"People underestimate the importance of listening."

"Sure do. I liked Bryan. My New York agent told me not to come to Hollywood."

"Well, you're here, and this is going to be a big film."

"I worry about the nudity and the nudity in *The Fan Club* test. I'm getting a reputation for only doing sex symbol parts."

"That's OK for now. You can work on that."

"They'll probably cut all my lines before the orgy and just leave the orgy in." (This is what the producers did.)

"Doubt that. First get your name out there. Penny did a small part in *Valentino* that had nudity and now she's up for *Coming Home*, the Ashby film."

"She's had more stage experience. She was in *Shenandoah* on Broadway. Nominated for a Drama Desk Award."

"She's had her share of heartache. Look, I was thrown off the set of *Lords of Flatbush* and replaced by Stallone. Didn't leave my bed for three days. Good news was it got me into transcendental meditation"

"Wish I could meditate." The waiter gave Richard the check. "What are you doing next?"

"There's interest from Terry Malick for *Days of Heaven*. Should be a good one."

"You do have to watch the sex symbol image, Richard."

"I worry about that, too. I've done plays for ten years."

"I remember you in *Grease* on Broadway."

"Went to London with that and became a member of the Young Vic in '73. I've paid my 'but-is-he-a-serious-actor-and-can-he-do-Broadway' dues."

"If this film takes off, you will have that sex symbol image," I said touching his hand, which felt warm and sensual.

"I can handle that."

We cuddled and hugged. He smelled fresh, like he had just stepped out of a shower. This was not the little boy Richard I had known in the early 70s. He had grown up. A man, he had a new appeal. He was considerate and comforting.

"Want to get together some evening?" Richard asked, his eyes glistening.

"When do you finish filming?" I asked, thinking making love with Richard might just be what I needed to forget Claude.

"Don't have to wait for that. Here's my address. Stop by." Richard wrote the number on the paper placemat, kissed me on my cheek, massaged my hand, and we left the restaurant.

That night I was alone with Tutu, my TV, and my Robert Mondavi white wine.

I finished the bottle, took a bath, threw on a yellow terrycloth robe, grabbed another bottle of wine, jumped into my convertible, threw the top down and drove to Richard's.

He opened the door. Holding the bottle of wine, I stood there in my robe and untied it. Barefoot and naked.

"Since I forgot the last time we made love, I wanted to refresh my memory," I said.

Richard laughed, grabbed the wine bottle, and carried me to his bedroom.

An agile, tender lover, Richard seemed unable to talk about his feelings—as opposed to being unwilling to.

Richard did not guilt me about being drunk, though he was completely sober. His gymnastic skills were apparent as he held me gently yet firmly and seemed not to want to let me go. Until the morning.

His eyes were riveting. His muscles taut. He was silent as we studied each other. Like Claude he wrapped his legs around my hips. He liked to be on top, in control, and he was good at it. He made me feel as though I were his leading lady. I imagined we were filming a remake of. *An Affair to Remember*. Bittersweet. He was destined for superstardom. In *Goodbar* his character was beautiful and predatory, slick and dangerous. Richard wasn't going to look back. I understood. He had said it. He had paid his dues. There was a sweetness to him even though I knew he was a player...his way. Most stars were.

I kissed his languid lips and didn't want to stop. But the alcohol was making my head spin while he remained coolly charismatic. Yep, he would be a big star, I knew. All of New York knew in the late 60s when the *NY Times* hailed him as one of the most talented newcomers off Broadway. He and Brad Davis. Two classmates from Wyn Handman's scene study were the sensation of Off Broadway.

And now he was in my arms. I had to let go of any desire to control Richard. He was an elusive sexual butterfly. Fiercely independent, intelligent and focused. He made love his way. Giving. His tongue ran over my body without hesitation. He didn't withhold. He was Valentino in the flesh. A sex symbol not to be forgotten. Not to be lumped with all the others, but to be remembered for his uniqueness. His thoughtfulness. His caring. But he was not Claude. I wanted to push all thoughts of Claude out of my consciousness, and making love to Richard helped me to do this.

Richard and I knew each other for fifteen years after this night, but we would never make love again.

In the morning he scrambled some eggs and served me eggs, toast, and coffee in bed.

"I have to run to be on the set," he said as he kissed me goodbye. "Sure wish we had scenes together so that we could see more of each other," he said, and he was out the door.

I stared at the closed door and wondered what Claude was doing.

In 1980, while visiting New York, I read Richard was starring in *Bent* on Broadway. He was playing a decadent, manipulative homosexual who tries to survive in a concentration camp and chooses to die rather than to deny his true self. He had won a Theatre World Award for his performance, but still bare-chested he was on the cover of *People* magazine as 'the reluctant sex symbol'. Feeling this image was damaging his career, he fired the press agent who gave *People* the bare-chested photo.

Since *Goodbar* Richard had starred in *Yanks*, *Days of Heaven*, and *Bloodbrothers*, but it was *American Gigolo*, about a sexually expert escort who serviced older women, that cemented Richard's image as a sex symbol. The film was about money and power and his role was about narcissism, self-love, and self-confidence.

By choosing to portray a homosexual in *Bent*, Richard was attacking his sexy image with fury.

After a standing ovation for Richard, I went backstage to say hello. He made time for me even though his family, who was warm and down-to-earth, was crowded into his tiny dressing room too.

"Richard, I want to tell you that I just discovered I'm an alcoholic." I said.

"That explains it!" he said with a wide smile.

"I haven't had a drink for a year."

"Congratulations." He stood and hugged me, then I excused myself and went home feeling proud that I was finally on the right track with my life. His awareness of the disease of alcoholism meant a lot to me. So did his approval.

Later I learned that there had been rumors that Richard was gay, but I never believed these rumors because of the good experience I had with him.

In 1983, I filmed *Take This Job and Shove It* and did a poster to promote the movie. One afternoon I was swimming at the Chateau Marmont, and I knew Richard was staying there. At the lobby, I dropped off a poster for him. He called later that afternoon.

"What a great poster! Is that you in the bikini?" he asked.

"Yes. And that's a movie I'm in."

"Do you drop this poster off with guys to get them to call you?"

"Don't insult me, Richard."

"I'm only in town a few days and would love to see you now."

"How about dinner?"

"I'm going to a movie with Paul Jasmine, but that's not until 7. It's 4 and I could be over in half an hour."

"Can't do that, Richard," I said. "Enjoy the film."

At first I was angry with Richard, who seemed to have become like many of the other stars I had come across. He especially reminded me of Jack Nicholson, who paged me for tea at the Beverly Hills Hotel. Then I realized the poster was highly suggestive and that I had given this message to him, though this had not been my intention. I forgave Richard for calling attention to my foolishly blatant display of flesh. Though it had been on paper, it still gave the wrong image.

Then I thought, "Sure I wanted him to see my beautiful, sexy poster, but why did he have to treat me like a sex object? ...everything that he had fought so hard for in his own career to avoid. How would he have felt if I had called him for sex when I had seen his bare-chested cover of *People* magazine? Is it that men don't care if they are treated as sex objects? Was his complaint about being viewed as a sex symbol only about his career, ego, and money? Even so, could he still view women only as sex symbols?"

After all he had played ferociously sexual characters in *Goodbar, Bent, American Gigolo*. Richard knew that sexuality was business in our profession. We had to sell it in our characters.

My poster was sexual because that was the image of my character in the film. My sexuality in my poster was business as had been my sexual image for my entire career.

Yet Richard could not separate respect for me from my image in my poster.

I had wanted to impress him with the fact that my photograph was representing a movie and thought he would be happy for me. Instead he wanted me to be a quickie, a matinee, and this hurt.

Still I am grateful to Richard Gere for having been there for me when Claude Picasso was not.

Malibu

It was the fourth of July in 1976 and everyone was looking for an A-list party. These historic events were cast and rated like everything else in Tinsel Town. An A-list party was an Absolute. Then there were the Bs for blunders and the Cs for calamites. One's self-worth was always challenged in Hollywood—if you took the town and its business, entertainment, for more than face value.

How to get invited to one of these swingin' shindigs? Through lots of phone conversations and name-dropping. If you acted as if you knew someone or something others didn't, you qualified for A-list parties. You became someone to fear because of your present—or potential—power.

Since the very early 1970s I had known Alana Hamilton, with whom I had ridden crosstown busses in Manhattan on "go-sees" for modeling. While she was not a success as a model, Alana became a successful celebrity wife when in 1972 she married George Hamilton, who was considered quite the catch. Alana studied Harold Robbins novels. Her mother, a drug addict, had tried repeatedly to kill Alana as a child, so Alana learned to defend herself at an early age. By 1976 Alana was unhappily married to George and in the process of divorcing. She wanted to meet new men. All the married stars stuck together. Quite often they had sex with one another. Celebrity wives kept a busy social schedule with their clique and watched like hawks on the prowl any new single women.

The celebrity husbands were kept busy so that they didn't notice that they were being manipulated by their frightened wives.

Alana knew I was single and circulating. I had told Alana about some of my adventures with stars. She enjoyed vicarious thrills and invited me to those cherished A-list parties hoping to meet men through me. Eventually she married Rod Stewart when she was several months with his child. Rod and Alana would have a stormy marriage.

In 1976, I considered Alana a good friend who tried to demonstrate her friendship by fixing me up with celebrity bachelors; however, I found most of them unappealing. They had lots of money, but that didn't conceal their gaudy Vegas taste. Besides, money was not the reason I was attracted to Claude. It was his animal sexuality and artistic heritage.

It was a hot, arid Thursday. We were due a heat wave for the weekend, with temperatures reaching the 100s. The beach, Malibu, was the place to be, but I hadn't been invited. Malibu's A-list invitations to luncheons and swim parties were cast like million-dollar picture deals.

I was committing the latest method of suicide by watching a four-hour tape of the current TV pilots. Hollywood's values and lifestyles were wearing me down. I wondered why I was in this God forsaken place, which had become a kind of prison. Hollywood reminded me of a town where flesh was peddled like meat at an open-air market where flies and bugs in the form of producers and directors crawled over raw flesh, sampling it and contaminating it. While I had fled France, Paris was looking like heaven after months of auditioning for people who treated women like cattle. I was beginning to miss Paris and longed for the life I could have had with Claude. Hollywood hadn't really been a choice. It had been a place I ran to after I could no longer model. I felt it was the last stop for me as far as supporting myself in a career. A town where producers, casting agents and directors told actresses to come to an audition for a role of a sex object and to dress for the part, but these women were truly auditioning for the bedrooms and the sexual fantasies of this male-dominated industry.

Picasso's Ghost

Suddenly the phone rang.

"Hi, Carole, it's Alana. Listen, what are you doing this weekend?"

"Oh, I don't know. I have a party up the beach in Trancas on Saturday, but I don't really want to go. What are you up to?"

"Well, Stan [Herman] and Linda [Evans] are having a party in Malibu on Saturday night. They only have room for fifty for dinner and you don't know them that well, but could you come for coffee? You know, they give the best parties."

"Sure, that would be great. Thanks," I said as I thought, "Pity I wasn't good enough to be part of the fifty." I had to be humble, though—much against my wishes.

"I don't know why you won't go out with Jim Randall, Carole," Alana said to me the day of the party. "Marisa Berenson will be there with Jim tonight. They're dating, but I thought of you first."

"He's not my type. I'm fussy and poor. I like artist types."

"Remember that in the unemployment line, dearie," Alana said.

At this time the actress Marisa Berenson was enamored with Jim Randall, a Beverly Hills rivet manufacturer and playboy. Marisa and I had modeled together. She reminded me of Paloma Picasso. Marisa's grandmother was Elsa Schiaparelli, and Marisa was related to the famed art historian Bernard Berenson. Marisa had been a favorite of *Vogue* editor-in-chief Diana Vreeland and was New York's most chic, elegant, well-bred model, but I never understood Marisa's taste in men.

Her sister Berry Berenson was a bit of a tomboy and became one of my best friends. Berry and her husband, Tony Perkins, and their two small boys had made me feel part of their family when I fled Claude.

Because of my friendship with Berry, I had taken Marisa, who was new to town, to some Hollywood studios and introduced her to producers. On 9/11 Berry Berenson would be one of the victims, aboard one of the planes that crashed into the Trade Center.

Alana had said this party on the Fourth of July would be an A-list party. What to wear? I chose a red, white, and blue paper jumpsuit from Fiorucci. But because it was paper, I could not wear panties under it as they would show.

I finished my makeup, grabbed a bottle of wine for the ride, hopped in my yellow Fiat, threw back the top, and drove off to Sunset Boulevard. The radio played "Satisfaction." At lights I sipped my wine. Why did I shake when I had to face crowds of strangers? I wondered if my father felt frightened like this when he had his tremors? When I hit Pacific Coast Highway, I began to move out at 80 MPH. Feeling the wind through my hair, hearing the Stones on my stereo, and seeing the moonlight shining on the ocean made me feel terrific. When I arrived at the party, I checked my makeup and again started to tremble at the thought of walking in. I had been told to come alone and was invited only for coffee. What would these guests think of me? I was being treated like dessert. But these people didn't know me well, I told myself. Alana was right. I shouldn't be offended. She knew how this town operated. I trusted Alana, downed the wine, and wasn't shaking anymore.

Walking in, I heard Donna Summers' "Love to Love You Baby." The bar.

Where was the bar? Oh, dear, there was Freddie Fields who just had cast me in *Looking for Mr. Goodbar*. Snuggled in a corner, he was looking dapper with his graying temples, faded jeans, single gold chain, and new red-headed wife. Ah, there was the bar. The house was covered in the romantic glow of candlelight. Everyone must be wondering why I was alone. Oh, why was the bartender so slow? I couldn't talk to these people. What would I say? God, give me a drink. I wanted to scream. The guests were reclining on sofas and pillows. They all seemed so relaxed. I smelled grass. Maybe that or the cocaine that was being passed made them all seem so confident.

The home was beautiful. The people were beautiful. And I was miserable.

One end of the living room was all glass and overlooked the ocean. I scanned the room for a familiar face. The guests seemed to be rich or famous, but were not my friends. I started to perspire and to tremble. Finally the waiter came with my drink

I missed Claude. The sea was shining in the moonlight, but it wasn't the Mediterranean or the bay at St. Tropez.

The smell of Jungle Gardenia almost bowled me over as someone tapped my shoulder.

"Well, there you are," Alana said, glowing in a conservative St. Laurent from a few years back.

"Who are these people?" I asked as the Stones screamed over the amplifiers "It's Only Rock 'n Roll."

"Oh, there's David and Dani Janssen, Polly Bergen, Marisa and Jim are off cooing somewhere. Liza Minelli's around. Joan Collins, David Niven, Jr. David Begelman's even here. With Gladys of course. But I really want to get my mitts on Jimmy Caan. My dear, he's such a hunk. Have you seen him?"

"Alana, I can't see a soul without my glasses."

"I gotta find George," Alana said. "I'll be right back."

I stood in the corner for about fifteen minutes watching and plotting how I was going to walk across the dance floor to the bathroom. This demanded courage and another drink.

The music was loud. The disco soundtrack from *Goodbar* blared, though the movie would not be released for another year. While my part was small, it had been coveted and was in one of the sexiest scenes in the film.

Donna Summer's disco beat incited everyone to dance. Almost with a fever. The guests were sitting on the carpet around the dance floor, which was jammed body to body. They could see practically up the dancers' skirts. I was glad I had worn a pantsuit...even if it was paper. It zipped up to my neck and had short sleeves and though it was tight, it had a sweetness to it—except when I moved. I stood in the corner watching others have fun.

Once again I missed Claude.

A few feet away a drunken Jim Randall danced. He was wearing gold chains, his shirt unbuttoned to the waist, displaying an abundance of curly black chest hair. While clutching a sober Marisa, Jim flailed drunkenly around the dance floor. As ridiculous as he looked, she remained the lady. She was beautiful, not because of her features, but because her persona was breathtaking. She had style.

I wanted to dance, too.

Someone grabbed my elbow. "Do you wanna dance?"

Thank God I had had plenty of wine. As the O'Jays sang "Backstabber," I began to dance. All my shyness, pent-up anger, and repression seemed to disappear. I was dancing with a stranger. So what? I wasn't rich or famous, but I could dance.

Out of nowhere an arm grabbed me around my waist almost crushing my ribs. I heard a THUD! Marisa lay on the dance floor with her legs spread and skirt up over her panties while screaming, "Help me, Jim. Where are you?" Her arms and legs waved in the air. She was on her back.

I looked into the face of the person who was clutching me and it was Jim Randall.

Ignoring Marisa's pleas, Jim grabbed me tighter by the waist.

"Let me go, Jim," I said, screaming. "Please, you're hurting me." He only smiled drunkenly and held me tighter. We were sliding and flailing around the dance floor. I was kicking him and hitting him, but the more I tried to free myself from his grasp the tighter he held me.

I felt the glaring stares of Freddie Fields, David Begelman and his wife Gladys.

Jim seized me fiercely.

Suddenly I heard a RIP. Something had torn. I didn't know what or where. Because of Jim's grasp, I was unable to look down.

"Please let me go, Jim, something ripped!" I said, begging. He pretended not to hear me. I felt a draft between my legs. Celebrities seated at our feet were staring at my crotch. Still Jim would not let me go. When I was able to look down, I saw my black pubic hair. Jim had torn about a ten-inch hole in the crotch of my jumpsuit. I began to hit Jim harder screaming, "Let me go! My jumpsuit is torn. You're hurting me."

I wished I was peacefully having tea with Grandmère in Paris.

All the guests were staring at us smiling while Marisa looked on, enraged.

Picasso's Ghost

The song ended. Jim fell drunkenly on the floor and passed out. When I saw my crotch and the enormous tear, I began to cry.

Linda Evans came running up. "Don't worry, Carole. It wasn't your fault. We all know that. Come upstairs and I'll give you something to wear. Everything will be all right."

In Linda's bedroom, I sat on the corner of her bed and quietly sobbed. She gave me some panties to put on.

Alana put her arms around me. "Carole, don't worry. Linda told me what happened. It will all blow over and Marisa will forget about it. Everyone will. But I've got to go find Liza. I'll be right back."

For about fifteen minutes while listening to the frenzy of "Don't Leave Me This Way," I waited for Alana, who never reappeared. I reached for a stale drink next to the bed. I drank it down quickly so that I could find the courage to leave. The scotch was warm and soothing, and suddenly the whole incident seemed rather silly and unimportant. I stood up. Looked into the mirror. Combed my hair and washed away any of Jim Randall's unwanted perspiration lingering from the heat of the dance. There. I looked better and felt better. Oops! I had slipped on the bathroom floor. It must have been wet. The bathroom smelled damp from all the salt air. I was a bit dizzy, but I'd be okay. Once I made it to my car, I'd be safe and away from these people and their A-list vibrations. The scent of another stale scotch permeated my nostrils. Sure enough, there was a glass in front of me on the sink. I finished it off and no longer cared what these people thought. FUCK 'EM. FUCK HOLLYWOOD A-LIST PARTIES. I had myself. And a new pair of Linda Evan's cotton panties.

Slowly I crept down the steps into the living room. Looking in Marisa's direction, I saw her gaze hatefully at me. I was too afraid to go up to her and talk about what had happened. Pointless. It wasn't my fault, but I could tell she wouldn't have wanted to hear this. What was I to do? Oh well, I thought, I'm OK, as I hiccupped and slipped through the crowd, making it safely to my little yellow Fiat that drove me at 80 MPH along the Pacific Coast Highway.

The road was sometimes a bit blurred, but I played the music loudly to keep awake and was so happy to be safe at the wheel. Well, I felt safe.

A half an hour later I pulled into my garage and passed out on my bed in my torn jumpsuit.

The next morning, I awakened with a terrible hangover and found my car parked in my neighbor's parking space. I hadn't remembered how it had gotten there and wondered why I hadn't undressed. I would have to cut down on my drinking.

War of the Wives

The next morning thoughts of the night before echoed inside my head along with my hangover. Should I call Marisa and apologize? What for? Maybe Alana would tell me how to handle this? She was smart with matters like this.

I would wait a few days before calling her.

"Thanks for inviting me on the Fourth, Alana," I said. "I'm real sorry about what happened."

"That was some evening. I don't think anyone will forget it. You left quite an impression. I didn't see what happened, but I heard about it the next day."

"What do you mean?"

"Marisa called and is very upset."

"Alana, I told you what happened. Did you explain it to her?"

"I tried. She doesn't want to hear it. She's freaking out about the whole thing Don't worry. It'll all pass. It's just her ego. Marisa and Jim are getting married."

"You're kidding. They just met."

"Not really. I introduced them last year. They were like lovebirds—until the other night."

"I thought they had only dated a couple of weeks."

"Oh, you know Marisa. When she wants someone, she usually gets them."

"What happened to David Rothschild?"

"She wanted to marry him, but he gave her a hard time. That's when I introduced her to Jim. She flew here for a vacation and to meet Jim. You know, I think he's divine. You, silly, were the first one I had in mind, but you wouldn't go out with him. You asshole. Anyway, Marisa did, as well as the rest, very secretly. Then she went back to Europe and the arms, or whatever, of David. She put more pressure on him to take her to the altar, or bank, but he still refused. So she came back to Hollywood and Jim. She said he was great in bed. Well, I knew that. So you missed out, Carole."

"You mean you've slept with Jim?"

"Oh, we just mess around from time to time, but not anymore. He's a great fuck. And you know he's loaded. Every airplane has to have some gadget he patented. He's very rich, my dear. That's why I wanted you to go out with him. But you're so fussy."

"So Jim and Marisa are really going to do it?"

"Wedding bells were in the air. Now they're a bit cracked after that party and your dance with Jim. Things will work out. Marisa likes all this attention and drama anyway. You know that."

"Yep, but I don't want to be her victim. What ever happened to Marisa and Rick von Opel? Wasn't she supposed to marry him?"

"That didn't work out either. He didn't want to."

"Why does Marisa want to get married so much?"

"My dear, the same reason as most women do. I haven't figured you out yet, but she has no money." I had never told Alana about my feelings for Claude and that I was waiting for him to set a wedding date.

"What? I thought Schiaparelli left lots to Marisa and Berry."

"I don't know details, but Marisa's piggybank is empty and she has an expensive lifestyle. Look for wedding bells very soon."

"God, this sounds like the makings of a mutual fund instead of a wedding."

"I try not to judge. Whatever makes them happy. Marisa has class. In that sense it's business, but they really do like each other. I don't know why you didn't give him a whirl. Sometimes you're so silly. Oh, there's George. I have to change Ashley's diapers before I see George or he'll kill me. Call you later."

With men I couldn't be calculating. Many a night I could have become pregnant by Claude and today would be a billionairess, but I didn't want to do this to Claude or to a baby. I thought too much of him of myself and of the baby to put him in the position of having to marry me. What kind of marriage would follow if Claude had to marry me? He would resent me and the baby. Years later she and Rod would divorce. Though Rod had wanted her to have a baby, had her becoming pregnant prior to marriage caused this marriage to end? No, I was proud that I had not forced Claude to marry me by getting pregnant. I was proud and poor, as Alana pointed out. I had fallen in love with Claude when he was poor. Yes, he had been famous and the son of Picasso, but there had been no chance of his getting to Picasso's wealth because of that Napoleonic Code.

Within a month word was spreading all over Hollywood that Marisa and Jim had set a wedding date. They had patched up their differences. The wedding was two weeks away and I still hadn't received an invitation. I didn't understand. Alana was supposed to have erased any bad feelings.

One day Alana and I were rehearsing the play *HeddaGabler* in her living room.

There was a knock at the door. It was Jim Randall, who had stopped by to visit George.

"Carole, I'm sorry about what happened on the Fourth," Jim said, sincerely. "That was very embarrassing for me. Please come to the wedding. Don't worry about Marisa. She'll cool down. It's her ego. She's being silly. You're part of our group and belong there. I want you to come. Consider yourself invited."

George Hamilton, looking very much the bon vivant in his well-pressed, newly purchased, faded jeans was discussing the details of the wedding with Jim. "Carole, don't let Marisa push you around," George said. "Just show up. Don't be as silly as she's being. Nobody will care about what happened on the Fourth. That's water over the dam. Sometimes I think Hollywood's one big reservoir that overflows from time to time."

"I'd feel better if I had a proper invitation," I said to Jim. "I really don't want to crash a wedding."

"Okay, I'll see that you get one," Jim said. "Now go on with your play, Mrs. Elvsted. Hey, Alana, so you're Hedda? Type-casting!"

"Shut up, you, douche bag!" Alana laughed.

The wedding would be in ten days and I still hadn't received my invitation. I called Alana.

"What's going on in Marisa's head, Alana?" I asked. "I haven't gotten an invitation, but Jim invited me personally. You heard him. I don't understand."

"Well, Carole, it seems Marisa thinks you fucked Jim on the dance floor that night and this is what she is telling people."

"WHAT?" That's ridiculous!" I said, shouting. "You were there and saw the whole thing! So was half of Hollywood."

"Frankly, Carole, I was upstairs when it all happened. You know that."

"I TOLD YOU WHAT HAPPENED!"

"Don't scream at me, Carole. This is between you and Marisa. I want no part of it.

She doesn't want you at the wedding and that's that. It's her wedding. What can I do?"

"Alana, you said you'd clear things up between Marisa and me. I'm terrified to call her. What good would that do?"

"I can't do the impossible, Carole. I tried, but she doesn't want to hear anything other than what she believes."

"That's unfair! It's not true!"

"I can't be responsible for what she says, Carole, and stop screaming or I'LL HANG UP. I have Ashley screaming all day long. My nerves are shot. I don't know what to tell you except don't expect to see an invitation from Marisa. I've got to go. Ashley's crying again, damn it! If I were you I wouldn't go to the wedding. You'd be a fool. Forget about it!"

I hung up and cried. I was being framed by Marisa, and blacklisted by the celebrity wives.

After a few days I called Marisa's sister, Berry, in New York. She'd clear it up. After all I was with her at the time of the birth of her two sons. And she was so kind to me after I left Claude.

"Berry, I don't know what's happening with Marisa. She's being ice cold and saying I had sex with Jim. Alana's the one who's had sex with Jim, not me. You know he's not my type. She's being unfair," I said, wiping my tears. "Can you talk to her for me? I don't think she'd take my call."

"Relax, Carole, and stop crying. Of course I'll call her. Sometimes she's a bit controlling."

"A bit!"

"I know. When we were little, we played the queen and her court. Guess who was queen. I'll call you tomorrow," Berry said. "Don't worry. I love you and Tony sends his love. Cheer up. This is all so silly."

The next day I waited for Berry's call, did not leave the house, and smoked a pack of cigarettes while polishing off a bottle of Robert Mondavi, my favorite white wine.

Berry and I had been friends for five years. I trusted her. I knew she'd straighten out the whole mess.

She never called.

A few days later I was rehearsing again with Alana and talked with George.

"Marisa's jealous," he said. "Come anyway. You should be there. You're part of the group. Jim is very fond of you and knows what happened. Don't let Marisa push you around. Just come."

Alana overheard George and started raging. "Carole, don't listen to him," she said, shouting. "What does he know about the wives of this town?" George coughed. "Don't cross your wires with them or you'll never be invited anywhere. I'm warning you." She put a kettle on the stove.

"Alana, you're ridiculous. Just stick to your herb tea. Marisa's simply trying to run the show." George smiled, calmly.

"Well, George, it's her show to run. It's her wedding." Alana popped a Niacin tablet.

"I don't think you should let her get away with this, Alana. Jim has all the money, is paying for the wedding for 800 people they barely know and he wants Carole there. She should come."

By this time I was shaking and confused. Going to the wedding could bring up all of the memories of my potentially looming wedding with Claude. Was it going to ever take place and if so what would it be like? Going to Marisa's wedding would help me to fantasize about Claude's asking me to marry him again and about the wedding we might still have. After all I did have the dress. I had been outfitted and was still ready to go.

After hearing the furor, Jack Martin, a friend and gossip columnist, called. Slight and nervous, beige in coloring but not temperament and armed with a sharp wit, Jack snapped, "Don't let her push you around. Over eight hundred people have been invited. Even people they don't know. Of course if they can help Marisa's career, anyone can come." Jack laughed in his high voice. "Look, it would be good for you to be seen at the wedding. You have a career, too, and should be out there with these people. Don't let her destroy an opportunity like this. Parties are big business here and weddings—even funerals—for Christ's sake!"

"You're right, Jack," I said polishing off a bottle of wine along with a hit of coke.

"I think you're silly not to go," Jack said, with an edge.

Marisa would just have to accept me at the wedding like I had had to accept her lie.

I was going to wear my wedding dress. The one Françoise Gilot had bought for my wedding to her son, Claude.

Dressed to Wed

Wearing my never-worn wedding dress to Marisa's and Jim's wedding for their eight hundred friends seemed like an appropriate choice. I was hoping Claude simply needed time to adjust to his new wealth before setting a date for our wedding. Maybe it would be good luck to wear this dress, which was exquisite—a salmon crepe de chine calf-length dress trimmed with shining sequins and pale pink beading, with a sheer bolero jacket worn over it.

I had bought some grass and cocaine for the affair. A few joints were going to help me get through this event and have fun. While I did my makeup, I sipped some white wine. My stomach was upset from nerves.

Looking into the mirror and applying my eyeliner, I remembered when my beautiful sister was crowned May Queen of her sixth-grade class. I was in second grade and busy running from boys who laughed at me because I was so skinny. They called me "toothpick." I always felt unpopular and disliked--especially by girls. Though I was the cheerleader with the most seniority, I never was chosen captain because the girls on the squad didn't like me.

My white wine wasn't doing the trick so I opened a bottle of Johnny Walker I had stashed in the kitchen cupboard for special occasions. I quickly poured some over ice and swallowed it. It tasted terrible, but maybe I'd stop thinking about the past. The past depressed me. Why now of all times was I obsessing about my sister and my childhood?

I grabbed the joints, stuck them in my handbag and swallowed more scotch. Jack was tooting the horn of his black Pacer—such an ugly car.

I ran out and hopped inside. "Hi, Jack. Oh, I'm so nervous. I don't know if I'm doing the right thing. What is Marisa going to say when she sees me?"

"Don't be silly," Jack said. "You have as much a right to be at this wedding as anybody. Half the guests don't even know Marisa or Jim. This is just one big party and business for everyone---including the bride and groom." Jack laughed, nervously. "You look beautiful. Forget about feeling unwanted. Nobody cares that much one way or the other, Carole."

Jack was telling me I wasn't that important. That I could understand. His words hit home. Maybe if I had some grass, I'd feel important. That's what I wanted. I liked Jack because he knew all the gossip yet he shared his scoops and secret information about others with me. I felt privileged.

"Besides, last night there was a bachelor's party at On the Rox and Alana and Marisa crashed it," Jack said, chuckling. "Hookers who had been hired—and not paid, mind you—ducked for cover when they saw Alana and Marisa. George kicked Alana but missed and his foot landed in a potted plant. Now he has a limp." Jack laughed. "You are hardly the focus of the wedding."

I took a hit from the joint. The grass smelled like freedom. It smelled like "I don't care." It smelled comforting. I needed to be comforted.

Why didn't Marisa like me? What was wrong with me? I couldn't talk about my feelings. I was too shy, too fearful, inarticulate, envious, blocked. And I didn't want to. Why would Marisa care? My sister never did. I had to hear my sister cared. But I could never tell my sister that I loved her either.

I was so confused.

Was this how wars began?

We were almost there. We were passing the Beverly Hills Hotel and about to turn off Sunset Boulevard. As we turned into Whittier, we became part of a long black line of limousines—mostly Cadillacs.

Picasso's Ghost

Our Pacer looked even sillier. What would people think if they see me getting out of this bloody black blob? Appearances are everything. Especially in Hollywood.

I had another hit of Mary Jane. I needed it to get out of this piece of shit on wheels in front of all these celebrities, the press, the cameras. Oh, God! How embarrassing! We were pulling up into the semicircular entrance. There was a marine blue Mercedes Benz stretch limousine in front of us and a Rolls Royce in front of that. Then a bunch of black buglike limos lined up like they were going to a funeral at Forest Lawn. If I were to marry Claude, I would arrive in one of Picasso's Hispano Suisses. That would put these nouveau riche to shame. What would Picasso think of this wedding? Of these people? In his youth he would have wanted to go, too. He was social. But later in his life he would have seen the folly in this event. Still, I was young and wanted to be a part of this circus and that's just what it was.

We had arrived. Oh, I knew no one would take my picture because I was getting out of a Pacer. I knew the wedding was starting off on the wrong footing. Thank God I had my coke tied to the lace of my underpants. The photographers ignored me. In fact one almost stepped on me. Drats! There was Ron Gallella. Ron was supposed to be a mean piece of work. Still I wanted him to take my photo. No way.

If I had been married to Claude, he would have taken my photo. Then the press could ballyhoo the name Picasso in the caption. I remembered when we were in Spain at a movie opening and Claude was seated between the film's star and me. The press had cut me out of the photo and had tried to make it look like Claude was dating the film's star. Oh, the press loved the name Picasso—and so did I. I had been cut out of the picture. Just like Claude was trying to cut me out of his life now.

Still I had an identity in Hollywood. The *Fan Club* test had given me some degree of fame. No, no one was taking my photo because of Jack. It was all Jack's fault and his lousy rotten Pacer. That was it! It was Jack's fault. Fuck Jack! I'll lose him and do some coke in the pantry.

We gave our wraps to a maid by the door.

"Jack, please excuse me," I said. "I'm nervous. I have to run to the ladies room." (To take a toot. TO TAKE A TOOT. I was screaming inside...you fool!)

"Forget yourself. It's all your negative thinking. I invited you. You have a right to be here. Get hold of yourself," Jack said, snapping again.

He was nervous, too. Jack was covering the wedding for gossip to be phoned in and written about throughout Hollywood, New York, Paris, London, Australia --the world. Jack was busy. He wasn't trusted by a lot of people, but I liked him—even if he was short with me from time to time--and even if he got gossip from me. That was his payoff. Jack could make me laugh and that was one of the most important things to me. I had to laugh—even if I was the joke.

I hit the bathroom and untied the coke vial from the lace string holding up my bikini panties.

AHHH. Sniff. Sniff. Better yet, one again for the left and one for the right. Now I felt like a Queen for a Day, at a Wedding, Bar Mitzvah, Confirmation, Mass, Requiem, Heavy-Weight Championship, Oktoberfest, Daytona 500, PTA, ERA. HURRAY! I felt great. Bring on the fools, the wedding, the wedding party, the guests. I was ready to suffer and to have fun at the same time. Now, I was laughing at the silliness of it all. Why had I been worrying about what people were thinking? Pablo Picasso wouldn't have worried. He would have understood why I wanted to be here.

Here I was worrying about people I didn't know. People I didn't like. And I cared what they thought. Well, fuck 'em! I was okay now. As long as I had my cocaine.

I didn't do coke in Paris. Never knew about it in Paris. Claude didn't do cocaine. This habit was taught to me in Hollywood by the A-list. Yep. How to fit in. Take a toot and it's all OK. Use it only for special occasions, I was told. Moderation. I couldn't do anything in moderation. Well, this was a special occasion. This was the kind of wedding I would have had with Claude. Might still have with Claude. How did I know what he was thinking? My fantasy had been to fly all my friends to Paris, have dinner at the Tour D'Argent—pressed duck all around. And I was wearing the dress I was to have worn to that wedding. The wedding of mine that never happened because I wasn't good enough for Claude. Maybe Claude would change his mind? Come to his senses?

But as far as these Hollywood A-list types—I wasn't good enough for them.

Marisa hadn't wanted me. Jim was just an excuse for her not to invite me. She simply didn't like me.

Just like Claude's family didn't like me. Françoise Gilot thought I wasn't good enough to be a Picasso. Paloma Picasso thought the same. Paloma didn't want me to have "that" name. No, no Carole Picasso for Paloma. With her marriage, she would have had to give up the name Picasso and use "his" name. She simply refused.

And truthfully, Claude resented me. Why? Because I had taken care of him when he was poverty- stricken...this to him meant that neither his mother or grandmother would support him. I bankrolled Claude —did their work--till he got to his father's billions. He used me as his parking lot, hotel, caretaker, all-day sucker. So did Françoise Gilot and Grandmère Gilot. They were all happy for me to take care of Claude so they could save their French francs.

Therefore Claude wore not only my ex-husband's clothes, but my clothes, was my househusband and today is a billionaire. People often resent those who gave them things like money, a home, and love when you were poor. I wasn't wanted by Claude or his family because they wanted to erase me with the past and that was why the wedding was, for the time being, not on the boards. But I could still hope. Claude left me dangling in Hollywood with a glimmer of hope and that kept me alive.

I left Claude before he had a chance to prove all this to me. I left him. He wasn't going to tell me I wasn't good enough. I showed him. I did. Suddenly I felt like crying. Coke, I needed more cocaine. Right. Left. Inhale! Ah, oh. Drats! Someone was pounding at the door. Time for the wedding, time for the entertainment, time for the clowns. Hollywood here I come...

The living room was swarming with celebrities, foreign accents, fancy gowns, costumes, light bulbs, and tacky furniture fortunately concealed by the more than eight hundred guests. I was on the lookout for the celebrity wives, headed up by Alana. I was sure they would be after me carrying hatchets, tomahawks, bows and arrows, diaphragms, vibrators, and dildos and were going to attack me right in the middle of the ceremony, ruining my wedding dress. My heart already was broken, so they couldn't hurt that.

I wasn't shaking anymore like I had been. The coke really worked.

"What took you so long?" Jack asked. "You missed so many stars."

"I was talking to the help. They don't think the marriage will last more than one year."

"Who doesn't know that?" (It lasted 18 months.)

Jack and I wandered into the garden passing Liza Minnelli, Halston, Valentino, Julie Andrews, Blake Edwards, Joel Grey, Jimmy Caan, Richard Harris, etc., etc. Conversations seemed to be in French and Italian about Marisa's wedding dress, designed by a beaming Valentino. Halston didn't look too happy, but he would have the opportunity to design Marisa's gown for wedding number two.

When we walked into the garden, I looked for the pool. There had been one somewhere, but I couldn't find it now because it was covered with flowers and a white leatherette altar. A huge tent was overhead, and I felt as if I were in the middle of the Super Bowl. Europeans with various shades of blue in their blood mingled with the biggest names in fashion, art, cinema, and finance. Football players, singers, producers, agents with toupees, musicians, writers, and actors. Andy Warhol was clicking away with his camera. Rona Barrett was hounding guests like Angelica Huston and Jack Nicholson for a television special on the event.

"Gogo Schiaperelli, also known as the Marchesa Caccia di Giugliano, and her second husband, Gino, trekked from Paris for the wedding of her eldest daughter, Marisa. "A sometime actress and full time beauty, 29-year-old Marisa was the regnant queen of the international jet set, who had found her king in the industrialist James H. Randall, 32," wrote the *NY Times.*

I wondered what the press would write if I were to marry Claude. British press had enthusiastically reported my love affair with Peter Sellers. Maybe Marisa could read about me. Claude and I still shared the apartment in the Sovereign together as well as Tutu (even if Claude occasionally kicked him). Why couldn't I stop thinking about Claude?

I looked around what had been the pool area and saw more than a hundred large round tables covered with glittering place settings, candles, and bouquets of white orchids. These tables supported guests whose chairs sank into the damp grass, sometimes spilling them out onto it. The grass was wet because of the pool's inadequate drainage system.

My hit of cocaine was beginning to wear off and the ceremony was approaching.

I would soon be running into the bride and the bridesmaids—all the celebrity wives.

"Jack, let's get another drink," I said.

"Get one. I'll be at Andy's table."

I quickly got a gin and tonic at the bar. A string quartet began playing classical music as guests were ushered to their seats. Jack had saved me a seat next to Andy Warhol.

"Hi, Andy," I said, my voice slightly slurred.

"Oh, hello, Carole, that's a beautiful dress you have on."

"Why, thanks, Andy. Excuse me," I said laughing. "This was my wedding dress, which I was to have worn with Claude. Françoise bought it for me."

"Oh, really?" Andy smiled. "It's so lovely. Who designed it?" he asked, flipping on his tape recorder.

"Karl Lagerfeld. We all went to Chez Chloe. Françoise, Paloma, and I went and picked it out one day…in May…and I've never worn it."

I felt better. Andy Warhol had paid attention to me.

I was beginning to talk myself into feeling superior to the whole scene, but when Marisa walked down the aisle, my ego was surgically removed. She looked gorgeous—shy, feminine, statuesque and vulnerable at the same time. If I were yet to marry Claude, would I look that beautiful? I wondered. She moved regally down the aisle. She should be a queen as well, I thought. But not of this lousy town. She's too good for Hollywood. This town could never appreciate her elegance. I did.

The bitch!

I guess everyone can't like you. I simply would have to accept her dislike of me.

After all, she wasn't my mother or sister. Or Paloma, though Marisa sure reminded me of her.

Grabbing the bottle of Dom Perignon in front of me, I refilled my glass.

Jim and Marisa were kissing. There was a flash of light; I waited for thunder. It was only the light from millions of cameras.

Ah, the wedding party was descending from the platform and beginning to mingle. God, I hoped I didn't see Marisa. I finished off the champagne and was getting dizzy. The wedding was so chic—except for the décor.

I missed Paris and Claude and Grandmère and Neuilly and tea in the carriage house. That was real sophistication and had heart. It was not this "Abby Rent's—I can get it for your wholesale" kind of chic. This was the pits. I wanted to get out...away. I was feeling dizzy and sick. Sick to my stomach and sick in my head.

I looked up. My feet were covered in mud from the faulty drainage system. I saw Marisa coming right toward me. She hadn't noticed me. Following behind the beautiful, elegant bride of everyone's dreams was Alana.

Marisa was a model bride. As I stared at her, my self-loathing and self-pity hit an all-time low continuing to haunt.

I was mesmerized. I only wanted to stare at her and to tell her I was sorry I had come and was sorry Jim had done what he had done. But it was too late for apologies.

The closer Marisa came, the harder I tried to look elegant, indifferent. That was what everyone else seemed to be doing. This was one of those relationships where money was the orgasm.

Claude and I loved each other before he became rich. Then everything changed. Our relationship had had soul and was based on family. Tutu was our baby. Françoise and Grandmère became my grandmother and mother and Paloma, my sister; my father became Claude's father. Picasso had been so cruel to Claude. So Claude was mean to me.

I was staring at George Hamilton, who was still limping from the bachelor party. Try to concentrate on George, I told myself. I smiled, but he seemed too busy to return my smile. He nodded. Why hadn't he come over to say hello? George had told me to come. Was he another celebrity husband run by his Hollywood wife, Alana? But he had always been nice to me. Besides, they were in the process of divorcing.

Oh, there was the groom, Jim Randall. I smiled and he hid his head like a little bad boy and then turned his back. Another newly anointed celebrity husband.

Marisa's eyes caught mine. Her expression was like a dying swan's. Poor Marisa. She looked so hurt and was so delicate. I couldn't help feeling sorry for her. She was so fragile.

Then I thought, "What? Am I CRAZY?" How could I have allowed her to trick me like that? She had manipulated me. What an actress! She had even been able to con ME. Suddenly she swirled around, turned on her heels and stormed away.

Alana came running up to me and said, "How could you have come, Carole?"

"Easily," I said and walked away. I grabbed Jack who was chuckling while holding his notepad and pencil. Andy Warhol had one hand over his face to hide his laughter and his other hand over the red light signaling record on his tape recorder, which had been busy all through the night.

"Let's go, Jack. I've had enough. Everyone's leaving and we don't want to be the last ones. Alana and Paloma taught me that."

We grabbed our coats. I reached for another gin and tonic for the road. "Jack, you were right and a good friend to insist I come," I said, sarcastically.

When I ran into my apartment, I pushed open the door to the bathroom, lifted the white toilet seat, knelt on the cold tile, and threw up. Tutu whimpered by my side and licked my thighs. Did he miss Claude? Was he trying to tell me this? How could Claude leave us alone in this town covered in tinsel while I was trying to grab onto each strand like a desperate lost soul. Trying to be a part of them when I didn't fit in. Like I didn't fit in with the Picassos. How had I gotten here? I had been a model, this was where I went wrong. Modeling was more flesh peddling. Before that I had been a schoolteacher. The children. What had happened to the children? My students? Their purity and innocence? What had happened to mine? I belonged in suburban Philadelphia. Not in Hollywood. Problem: I had needed to pursue acting. When I left Claude, I needed an income. When I had tested for *The Fan Club*, my wise agent, Ruth, had said, "Don't move to Hollywood." She had been right. I didn't fit in. Hollywood was not a home, but a place where my body was parked until Claude set a wedding date. A place where an actress was chained naked to a bed, filmed, and then--as this test was passed around the party circuit of this town--told this test was art.

There is no business like show business. I understood why Peter Sellers hated Hollywood's values.

As I slowly stood up, I pulled part of my skirt out of the toilet. I was too drunk to see or to care that it had fallen in.

I stumbled onto my bed, crawled out of my dress that smelled of vomit and dizzily curled up on my side. Now how could I wear it to my wedding? While hugging a pillow between my chest and knees, I cried.

I wondered why I had gone to the wedding.

I wondered if Claude was ever going to marry me.

I wondered if Claude was going to jilt me.

Darkest Hour

After the wedding I resumed my acting career and filmed an episode of *City of Angels* with Wayne Rogers. I played a nun. The director tried to seduce me in my habit. After studying acting for about five years, this was demeaning.

Alana and I began studying comedy improvisation in Harvey Lembeck's workshop with classmates such as John Ritter, Robin Williams, and Marylou Henner. We had fun and sharpened our comedic skills.

I went on to film a segment of *All in the Family* in which I played a pregnant woman who instead of going to an obstetrician mistakenly goes to a veterinarian. "You have talent as a comedian," Carroll O'Connor said. I knew it was my classes with Harvey Lembeck that were teaching me timing.

Work was diverting me from my focus on Claude's call and our impending move out of our New York apartment.

On May 19, 1977, Claude called. He said he wanted to give up our glamorous, all-glass apartment in the forty-eight-story Sovereign as the lease was up. He would be arriving on May 22. I flew to New York and to prepare for his arrival ordered six custom-made shirts with his monogram from Brooks Brothers. When Claude arrived, he had no present for me.

When he put his arms around me, I forgot my resentments. We kissed. His lips felt like cushions of love and he carried me into the bedroom where we opened the boutique. His touch felt soothing and comforting, but his words were empty.

Carole Mallory

"You look good, Carolina. Hollywood is agreeing with you," he said while I wondered whathefuck? I was awaiting a wedding ring. Not flattery. And certainly not a compliment about my life in Hollywood that along with fleeting moments of triumph was fraught with despair.

"We'll stay in the St. Moritz Hotel for the move if that's alright with you," he said.

"Are you still dating Peter Sellers?"

"No," I said. "Who are you dating?"

"Oh, there was that model you thought looked like Vivian Leigh. Anna. She moved in and tried to get pregnant. So I threw her out."

"How did you meet her?"

"At a fashion show for St. Laurent that Paloma dragged me to."

"So Paloma introduced you to her?"

"More or less."

"Cute," I said.

We were together in Manhattan for one week. Each day Claude went to see lawyers and art dealers while I was to stay in the apartment, pack our possessions, and arrange the May 22nd move.

On that day I was heartbroken. Dividing up property gave a permanence to our breakup that Claude's lips betrayed. I had been waiting for a wedding ring to be slipped on my hand. Instead I was being kicked out of a home we had shared. Feeling devastated and worthless, each morning at the St. Moritz when Claude donned one of my Brooks Brothers shirts that I had bought with my unemployment and my savings from my more successful modeling days, I began the habit of dialing room service, ordering whiskey, and taking Valium. In my confused and tortured mind, I was determined to hurt myself and getting drunk and taking pills was one way. Since Claude had refused to marry me each time I had sex with him, I had felt as though I were auditioning for him. So I turned the tables when I ordered whiskey each morning, took pills, and drank enough to pass out.

Sex between Claude and me had been fantastic. So why hadn't he given me that engagement ring he had bought for me? He was treating me like a whore. Worse than a whore. Whores were at least paid for their services. I was being jilted for my years of servicing and supporting Claude. Yes, I was being jilted because he had wanted to marry me in Paris, had bought me an engagement ring, but had stalled about setting the wedding date. My father had tried to commit suicide so I had to leave Claude in Paris to see my father who was in a hospital in Philadelphia. But now that sex felt right between us, I assumed Claude would want to marry me again, but he didn't mention this. Was it because I had been sexually inadequate and he had said he liked the sex just to placate me? Was he manipulating me to get rid of me? Was this a legal trick he had learned from being around all those lawyers? Had those lawyers been saying, "Make it look like she left you or she can sue you for being jilted"? Did I need to have sex with more men to learn how to be a good lover? Would Claude then set a wedding date? I was full of questions, some wild and others all-too-real.

No, I hadn't taken care of him and fallen in love with him for his money because when we met he had none and there had been little hope that he would see any of Picasso's billions because of the Napoleonic Code. But now that his mother had won her over the code and Claude had become a billionaire, I felt it right that he reciprocate the kindness and generosity that I showed him in having supported him. Now he had wanted to have sex, but did not want to honor his commitment to me. Were his lawyers advising him to have sex with me to confuse me? We had been engaged. But why didn't he set a wedding date?

Was it because I was bad in bed? That could have been it, but it also was because I wasn't good enough out of bed. This was the real reason. In his eyes I was common. Claude, now that he had become a billionaire, wanted someone from a family that had class. I was a farmer's daughter. Though my father was blue-blooded, a relative of Civil War Hero General Lou Wagner, who led the Battle of Bull Run, my deformed, mentally ill father had been an accountant. Why would Claude's family care about Civil War heroes? We weren't good enough for the Picassos. We were a part of the working class. Well, maybe the working class would appreciate my sexuality. Since I wasn't good enough for Claude and the Picasso family.

In Picasso's eyes Françoise Gilot's family was bourgeois. A Communist, in his later years, he preferred the working class.

Picasso would have appreciated me. In Vaularis he met the local potter's daughter, Jacqueline Roque, and married her. Françoise and her children, Claude and Paloma, had been raised to look down on Jacqueline as common. And I suspected this was how they viewed me.

One night Claude and I were invited to Tavern on the Green for a party for *Good Housekeeping* magazine given by actress Deborah Raffin and publisher Michael Viner, but Claude would not go. He knew press would be there. Claude hated the press. Michel Viner was furious that I did not bring Claude and threatened to terminate our friendship, but eventually he forgot his threat. Michael was a good friend who introduced me to many Hollywood celebrities, but he loved publicity. (Michael Viner became the publisher of Phoenix Books and later became my publisher for *Loving Mailer*, my memoir about my relationship with Norman Mailer.)

The next day Claude did give a speech about his father at the Whitney Museum.

Dr. Joyce Kootz, a foremost psychologist and wife of Picasso's most successful American dealer, Sam Kootz, listened by my side to Claude's talk. Afterward she said, "Don't give up your career. It is important for your identity that you work." I wondered what Dr. Kootz had heard in Claude's speech about Picasso that caused her to warn me about Claude and my choices in life.

I now think I know. It was impossible for me to see what was happening back then. Claude loved to talk about his father. Though when he met a stranger, he would state the opposite, within five minutes he would be recalling his childhood. This was all he could talk about--with strangers. He had to set up his relationship with his father. The stories were those filled with love and humor. Then he would get that blank, almost oriental smile and glaze over his eyes.... Still, when he flashed his smile, my world lit up.

Claude was very emotional and had a fiery side to him that I adored. The Spanish was there. I suppose I confused that with strength. For a couple of years I had loved him unconditionally.

But this love turned to fury in May at the St. Moritz Hotel. Ordering whiskey each morning from room service and taking pills was my way of getting revenge for what I felt he was putting me through. Throwing me out of my home. Throwing me back to Hollywood, that cesspool of corrupt human values. Where I would be tossed around like one more actress auditioning for the male-dominated power structure who saw women as receptacles for their prurient pleasures. I was angry that I had to return to Hollywood. After my stay with Claude in New York, I threw myself back into work as best I could while my drinking escalated.

On July 18, 1977, Claude wrote me. "It has been nearly impossible for me to express what we had while we were in NYC. Wonderful is rather banal, extraordinary is rather pedestrian. Magic I don't believe in. It had to be us. I started a few letters. They turned out to be useless efforts of trying to convey things and warm feelings that can only be understood as such.----Words seem to make all of it so flat. What prompted me to write today is that I dreamed about you last night."

In the summer of 1977, Françoise Gilot phoned me in Hollywood from her home in La Jolla.

"What a surprise," I said, stunned that she would call. "It's good to hear from you."

"Carole, I'd like to take you to lunch this Wednesday. I will be in L.A. then. Are you free?" she said in her high, thin voice.

"Why, yes," I said, falling onto the bed.

"We'll go to Ma Maison. I always feel comfortable there. See you around 11:30?"

"Yes, how are you and Jonas?"

"Oh, we're fine. And you?"

"OK, how's Claude?

"He's good. We can catch up at lunch."

"Thanks for calling."

I sat on the bed and wondered what Françoise wanted from me. What had I done now? Françoise never did anything without a reason. Though she had given me the Picasso jewelry and had bought my wedding dress, I never thought that she liked me, more that she tolerated me.

As I walked into Ma Maison, I was nervous. All heads turned. They always did. That's why everyone ate here. To see and be seen. It was a fashionable restaurant frequented by the movie crowd. At this time there was no roof over the terrace and the outside was like a garden, despite the Astroturf. Pink linen cloths covered each table and there were fresh flowers and umbrellas saying Cinzano, Evian, Perrier in bright primary colors. It had the feeling of a circus, but only for celebrities and the rich.

Patrick Terrail was the owner as well as the maitre d' and was a good friend of Françoise. His father owned the Tour D'Argent in Paris. Patrick greeted me with a smile. "Hello, Miss Mallory," he said. "Françoise is waiting for you." I loved Patrick. He was a kind and gentle man. He took my elbow and walked me to the table.

Françoise's face brightened as she kissed me on one cheek then on the other in the French manner.

"It is good to see you, Carole. You look lovely as ever."

"Why, thank you, Françoise. You always do." I was glad we had finished with the formalities and could get down to the reason she wanted to talk with me. I thought she was beautiful, but I didn't like the way she dressed. This day was no exception. She had a print jacket over a skirt of a different print. She was so confident in herself that it was apparent that she didn't care what people thought about such matters. Not trying to look provocative, which was my usual attire, I wore a conservative black pantsuit with a white silk shirt.

"Carole, I want to talk to you about Claude." My heart jumped. "We drove through Switzerland this summer and were able to talk to one another. You know how private he can be. He told me you were the one woman he has always loved."

I began to cry. "What happened to Anna?" I asked, referring to the model whom Paloma had introduced him to. I knew he had told me that he was no longer seeing her, but I wanted to hear what Françoise had to say.

"Oh, that was over a long time ago." Françoise smiled. Françoise rarely showed her feelings and had difficulty expressing warmth. Her words were loving; her demeanor, cool. Picasso's cruel treatment of her and the devastation she suffered after walking out on him could have been the reason for her fear of revealing affection.

I couldn't see through my tears.

"He's on his way here from Japan and will be calling you shortly. I think you two should get married and stop this foolishness. I want to help."

"Françoise, I don't believe this. I've never wanted to tell you, but when I left Claude, I said, 'You're doing to me what your father did to your mother. You're forcing me to leave you just like your father forced your mother to walk out on him.' Claude shouted, 'No!' and put his fist into the wall."

Françoise held my hand and we wept together.

I never had known Françoise cared.

This was the last time I saw Françoise Gilot, who, as it turned out, so wanted me to be her daughter-in-law.

A few days later the phone rang.

"Claude, where are you?"

"Tokyo."

"My, you do get around."

"Yep, I'll be in L.A. in a week. Françoise told me you had lunch. Do you want to see me?"

"I think I'm free."

"Can you meet me at the airport?"

"Of course," I said. "Tutu and I will be waiting for you."

"Do you want anything from Japan?"

"I'd love a kimono."

"See you in a week. Are you still my *petite bébé*?"

"What do you think?"

"Keep your boutique open."

"And you watch your shopping. Don't spend too much. Save some for me."

We blew kisses and hung up as I opened a bottle of wine and cuddled Tutu.

"He's coming to see us, Tutu," I said, wiping away my tears.

This week I hired a maid to clean up the apartment, to polish the silver and to make everything sparkle for Claude's arrival. A sitcom had wanted to cast me, but I refused the work as I had to prepare for Claude. The gym became my daily haunt. My hair was cut and colored, and my nails were done a bright red, Claude's favorite color.

While preparing my apartment I thought back to those wonderful weekends we would spend in Easthampton outside of New York at our friends' Janice and Hale Allen on Further Lane. They had class. They made Claude and me feel welcome each weekend, when we drove out from the city with them in their beautiful blue Bentley convertible. They were fun and kind to Tutu as well, who of course always came with us. Lunching on the beach in front of their Easthampton home was a kind of existence that Hollywood knew nothing about. Simple. Steeped in country chic— fresh vegetables and various jellies and jams. Janice even gave a bottle of jam as her Christmas present. There were no stars on the beaches in the early '70s. No Hollywood values dictating, "Look at me! What can you do for me?" No plastic surgery. No makeup. Fresh country air. Claude would photograph me in their outdoor shower. He loved to take pictures of the countryside and of Tutu and me.

Then there were Tony Rosenthal, the artist, and his wife Halina, who had a home in the Springs. Tutu would run around his sculptures on their lawn, lifting his leg on the bronze, just as Picasso's children had learned to piss on the sculpture of the goat outside his villa in Cannes to give it patina.

Claude and I had good friends together and there was always the feeling of family that came with these memories. Family and simplicity.

The Hollywood I had come to know had none of these qualities. I did not want to stay there without Claude, but where could I go? I couldn't go back to modeling. My New York home was gone. I had to stick it out in the jungle called Hollywood unless Claude asked me to be his wife. There was still that possibility. He just needed time, I told myself. Time.

Then I remembered the night at the gala at the Museum of Modern Art when we got into a fight. We had been dancing wildly like the night we met at that disco, Hippopotamus. My skirt was in the air and we were photographed raging at each other. But we made up. We always made up. Would we make up this time?

Then there was that party for Diana Ross where they photographed us. My hair was piled high on my head and I towered over

Claude, but it didn't matter. He never minded that I was taller than him. At least he never told me that he did. Maybe this had been one of our problems after all. Claude resented that I was taller than him. No, that wasn't it. Claude just resented that I had taken care of him when he was poverty-stricken.

This was our inescapable problem, I realized. I had known him before he became a billionaire. Before he could pretend to take Picasso's place. Before he could pretend to be Picasso by caring for Pablo's' possessions. Before he could believe he was Pablo Picasso incarnate.

The day of Claude's arrival Tutu and I waited restlessly at the airport. There he was. Tutu began to whimper. Claude's eyes caught mine. He dropped his luggage and held me while Tutu squealed with joy and pulled at Claude's trousers. Claude felt so good. I felt safe with him. We embraced and it was as though he had never left my arms. All that victimization—by the *Fan Club* test, by Marisa Berenson, and by the players of Hollywood's casting couch—faded into the distance. When Claude held me, I felt as though we were one. We didn't talk. We cried.

Had he been having sex with women in Paris? In Japan? Geishas? It didn't matter. He was now in my arms.

"Let's go home," I said to Claude. "It's time to open the boutique."

I was driving my Fiat when at a red light, he said, "Guess what I have for my little chickadee? Ta TA." He smiled as he pulled out of his suitcase a navy and white cotton kimono and a print of a bamboo leaf. A *cotton* kimono! I didn't know the Japanese made cotton kimonos! The only kimonos I had seen and had owned were silk! Still cheap, I thought and I still loved him.

But I was hoping for that engagement ring he had told me that he had bought for me. A painting by Picasso. A sign that he cared.

When he held me in his arms and we made love on my living room carpet next to his suitcases, I forgot about the cotton kimono, the engagement ring, the painting by Picasso. I didn't vacuum the carpet.

We held each other and cried some more.

His lips were still those sensuous messengers of love. His small hands touched me like never before. His palms caressed my naked skin as though I were Picasso's favorite sculpture needing a gentle dusting. "Let me see your iron breasts, my *cocotte*," he said with his half smile as he gazed at Angela and Katy. *"J'adore* ta titties." "Have you felt many others, Claude?" I asked, wondering about his fidelity.

"Oh, a few, but none like yours. When I've been with a woman, I was always reminded of you. You haunt me, Chérie. You and the taste of your *langouste*. Did you allow other men to feel you like this?" Claude asked while kissing the nape of my neck.

"A few, but only out of loneliness for you."

"You say that now."

"I say that now and forevermore. You are the only one for me, Claude."

"And Peter Sellers?"

"He was just to pass the time."

"Still can't read a book?"

"Peter was fun, but not the lover you are."

"I'm sure there were others."

"I was trying to use men to forget you. Let's not talk about them. We're together now and that's what counts."

"But I'm going to have to go back to Paris."

"I'll wait for you, Claude."

"Let me hold your *fesses*, that nook just above it. Those dimples I love. Let me see your mound of Venus. Brush it against my thigh like you do so well. I want to taste your *langouste*."

"I want *ton zizi*,"

He pressed himself in me rhythmically. Perfectly. Slowly. Then rapidly. Then slowly. Then quickly. I felt him grow bigger and bigger, wider and wider. Now Claude was on top of me, his eyes staring into mine. Possessing me. Claiming me. Stealing me away from all the badlands of Hollywood. Taking me back to that Paris I had hated and now missed. I missed it because it reminded me of Claude. He even smelled like Paris, part tobacco, part aftershave. He wore Guerlain's Habit Rouge. I still have his bottle of it.

I still have a bottle of Mille by Jean Patou that he had bought me in 1974. I'm still saving it. For what? Memories. When I smell it, I think of Claude and the last time we made love on my carpet in the Lotus Apartments in West Hollywood. It had been Valentino's country home. It was steeped in history and now would have Claude Picasso's sperm on its carpet, adding to nostalgia.

"Je vien, Chérie," Claude said, shouting. I reached for his *ruppettes* and gave them a scratch or two. Then he let out a scream and so did I. We had come together. I imagined time had stopped and Claude had not left my side.

"It's as though we've just met," he said through tears. "It's like the when we first made love." He smiled that little boy smile that I loved so.

"That night outside Carnegie Hall," I said. "You haven't changed."

"Are you kidding? Look at my hair? It's missing on top. I want a transplant."

I began sobbing all over again. "And I still love you, Claude."

"Why aren't we happy in Paris when things are always wonderful between us in America?"

"I don't know. Maybe I don't travel well—like a vintage wine," I said, pouring from a bottle of PouillyFuisse into his glass, which I had Windexed clean.

Then he reopened my boutique. We had a rummage sale and within no time Claude put everything right where it belonged. Claude kissed me there like no other man. He knew how to give me my own erection. For me Claude was more handsome than any of Hollywood star. He should have an agent, but NO. Then he wouldn't be mine and I didn't want to share him anymore. It was too painful to think of his being with other women while I was running to other men just so we could forget each other. This didn't make sense. Was this the price of becoming a billionaire? Being separated from those you love so that you can organize your assets? When we were holding our most valuable assets in our arms at this moment? All that material junk was just that. Claude cried and I cried, and it was over. We held our wet shaking bodies and fell back on the floor and stared at the ceiling. Tutu scratched at the bedroom door. I opened it and we three held each other by Claude's suitcases. Our family was united.

I felt wonderful and had fallen in love with him all over again.

"Do you remember when we first met?" he said.

"How could I forget?" I said.

"When we danced," he said.

"I love you," he said.

"I've met someone who reminds me of you," he said. "Only she likes Paris."

At the airport when Tutu and I said *au revoir*, Claude kissed me with those tender lips, looked at me with his sad brown eyes, and pulled me tightly against his chest as though he would never let me go. Then with a half smile he said, "Maybe I'll call you and we'll get married in Vegas, *bébé*."

Claude returned to Paris. He married that someone who reminded him of me.

When I realized I had been jilted, I tried to forget Claude and my broken heart by having affairs with many men. Françoise had been a mistress of Picasso, the genius, and from 1983 to 1991, I had been the long time companion of Norman Mailer, a genius.

Not long after Claude married, I bottomed out as an alcoholic. I ended up with a rock-and-roll clothing designer who would beat me up until my therapist saw the bruises and said something.

"I was just drinking some wine. I'm chic."

"Well your bruises aren't.'

She sent me to a doctor at St. John's Hospital who asked me 20 questions about my alcohol use. I had more than three yeses.

"Well, you're an alcoholic,' the doctor said.

My therapist arranged for a celebrity to take me to my first meeting. He was not anonymous. His name was Gordon MacRae. *Oklahoma* echoed in my consciousness. Thoughts of cornfields, farmhouses like the one my mother was raised in had become imbedded in my consciousness, and Gordon reminded me of that. My past that I had been ashamed of had become something I was

Picasso's Ghost

now proud of. I wanted Gordon to be my sponsor. He could not do this as women need women sponsors, but he said, "I'll take you to meetings—but only if you don't drink."

And so I got sober for Gordon MacRae. In time I learned to stay sober for myself.

Norman Mailer and Me

Dawn and Beyond

In the summer of 1980 in an old Episcopalian church used for AA meetings, I sat teary-eyed as an elegant Irish woman told the group about her dog's death.

"When my dog died, he had led a full life," she said. "I knew his death was meant to be."

She told a room filled with perhaps fifty recovering alcoholics about her life and calmly referred to herself as once having been a starlet. She was laughing. Inside I was screaming. After eight years I was still trying to become a star and refused to admit the fact that I was a professional starlet. I wasn't laughing. I wasn't funny.

That night my high hopes of being discovered by Hollywood ended.

After the meeting, I shook the woman's hand and thanked her for being the speaker. "I loved what you shared about your dog. I have a tiny poodle named Tutu," I said. "I'm so afraid he might die soon. I don't think I could handle it. He's been with me nine years and is like my baby."

She put her arms around me and gave me her handkerchief.

"Is your dog alive today?"

"Yes," I said, nodding.

"Then today you have nothing to worry about. Stay in the NOW. The future is suicide and the past is death. Now is all we ever have." She held my hand firmly while I stared into her ice-green Irish eyes. I heard her strength and could see it. "Call me." She smiled as she gave me her number. "Don't worry. I'll help you and so will this program---if you let us. Just keep coming back."

Was I crazy and dreaming this whole experience? She was what I wanted to be. I could never be strong like that. Her strength was magical. I believed her.

I went home and held Tutu. If he were to die, I would be alone. I never wanted to be alone. Stay in the NOW, I told myself. Tutu was alive and well and so was I. I kissed his little wet brown nose, looked into his eyes and realized that at this moment I had nothing to worry about. I turned on the TV and sure enough there was Hitchcock's *Rebecca*. Great! I snuggled with Tutu and soon we fell asleep.

A few months later I was barefoot while vacuuming when I stepped on something damp. Looking down I noticed a foamy spot, then another and as I walked to the bathroom, I discovered another. Tutu was lying on the cold ceramic tile looking up at me with white foam oozing from the sides of his mouth. I held him. He was trembling and damp all over. Within minutes we were at the vet.

Dr. Miller kept him all day. "Come back this evening," he said. "I'm going to pump his stomach and give him medication to sleep. Don't worry. I think he'll make it through the night. He really needs a good long rest. If he has trouble sleeping, call me. I could keep him here, but he does better with you. You are connected in a very strange way. I think his love for your is the best medicine he can have now."

I held my baby telling him, "*Ça va, mon petit Tutu. Tu va etre mieux. Je t'aime.*" Claude had taught Tutu French nine years ago when Tutu was a puppy in Neuilly.

That night I watched Tutu closely, giving him medicine every four hours. He didn't want it. Instead he lay curled up in a corner breathing heavily. He didn't close his eyes, but stared at me with them half opened to make sure that I didn't go anywhere. He seemed restless and kept hobbling into the bathroom to lie on the cold tiles. After a few minutes I followed while asking him, "*Qu'est-qui ce-passe, mon petit? Tu va etre mieux à demain. Tu va voir. Mama*

Est ici. Ne te trouble pas."

I carried him back to the bed and laid him on the floor next to it, hoping he could rest.

"*Bonne nuit*, Tutu," I said. "*Dors bien. Je t'aime avec tout ma coeur.*" He opened his eyes, showing that he had heard me and loved me. Unconditionally. He was telling me that he loved me more than Claude had loved me, more than my mother, my sister, and more than any star, more than any man I had made love to, and better than any human being ever could.

We both went to sleep and waited for the Sandman. When I was little and sick with rheumatic fever, each night my mother had to pat me to sleep as we awaited the arrival of the Sandman carrying with him a peaceful night's sleep.

In the middle of the night I smelled a foul odor. I looked down at Tutu. He was fast asleep. Maybe I was dreaming.

In the morning I rolled on my side and looked down at Tutu, who was still asleep. He hadn't jumped on the bed like he usually did. I reached over to pet him and to give him his good morning kiss.

His body was ice cold and stiff. I grabbed him, pulling him toward me to kiss him.

He didn't move. His legs were outstretched in a walking position. His eyes were sealed. He had a peculiar odor. He was hard as a rock. He was dead.

I ran my fingers around his mouth, pushing his gums over his teeth, hoping he'd make a face and pull away in disgust. I held his stone-like body on mine and cried, kissing him for a long time. Around noon the phone rang. It was Heather.

"Tutu's dead. He died in the night," I said through tears.

"What? What are you going to do?"

"I don't know. Nothing. I'm holding him now."

"I'll be right over."

I left the door open and returned to my bed and to Tutu's body. I didn't want to let him go—even though his spirit had gone. I couldn't let go of what he had left behind. He always had been there to lick and to comfort me when I was in pain and I wanted to do the same for him. He had gone with me on all my overnights with lovers—even stars. No one was too rich or too famous for Tutu. He visited Rod Stewart when I was too shy and too afraid to go alone that first night. Then I remembered the horror of having to check him with the coat check woman at Maxim's because I had forgotten to check the Michelin Guide and Maxim's was *Pas de chien*.

Tutu had given me courage. He was Supertoots and as I lay in bed I thought, "Maybe he could still be here for me, but in a different way. Maybe I could still talk to him and feel his nose against my ear, hear his whimper when he laughed at my jokes and keep these feelings close to my heart. As long as I lived, he would live too—inside of me instead of outside of me. In a strange way maybe we will be even closer.

Heather walked into the bedroom. "Carole, let's take him to the vet," she said as she wiped her tears. "I'll call the vet and make arrangements. Why don't you get dressed?"

"I'm going to wear this. I don't need to put anything else on. I want to wear what I had on last night when he was alive." My long black jersey dress was covered in holes from Tutu's favorite game, *"joujou."* Tutu loved the taste of this dress. His attachment to it brought back memories of a blanket I used to suck when I was a baby. Mother used to wash it in some wonderful detergent. I had to take it everywhere. Sucking it relaxed me. It was light blue and had little white animals trimming the border. It was called "Blankie." Maybe the animals trimming the border were poodles. That's how I would think of it. I understood Tutu's obsession with certain pieces of clothing. This obsession ran in the family.

I placed Tutu's cold body on the bed and went to the desk for a pair of scissors.

Heather looked alarmed. "What are you doing?"

"I want to cut off some of Tutu's hair and keep it."

She looked away.

From his ear I cut long strands of curly dark brown hair. It looked like lamb'swool. I placed it in a stationery box and put it in the top drawer of an English chest Claude had given me. This way Tutu's memories would be protected by Claude's memories. I haven't opened the box since Tutu's death.

"Dr. Miller said he would make arrangements, Carole. Would you like that?" Heather said.

"Yes, his body's not important now."

Within minutes Heather was helping me down the stairs. I was carrying Tutu rolled in a red wool blanket I had stolen from TWA on that last flight from Paris when we both left Claude, his master. The stewardess and crew had been so nice to him. I took a photo of him with his head jutting out of his doggie crate while seated on the armrest watching the movie.

Then there were the phone calls he got in French from friends. Richard Lindner, the artist, was one of his admirers. Françoise and Grams also would talk to him over the phone.

Tutu had been around. Like me. He had pissed on Picasso's grave, all of Picasso's chateaux, on the grounds of Versailles, Fontainebleau, the lawn of the Salk Institute, where Washington crossed the Delaware when I did my plays in New Hope, Mom's farmhouse in Shoemakersville.

In Paris he had been served the *plat du jour* Chez Lipp and he eavesdropped when Grandmère taught me French and I tried to teach her English. In response to French commands he was able to cross the streets of Manhattan—without a leash—and never once came close to danger.

Tutu was the baby I always wanted, but was afraid to have. I knew I was irresponsible. I never felt I'd be a good enough mother. As it turned out, I think Tutu had died of Parvovirus because the vet hadn't given him his second shot to prevent it. I could blame the vet, but it had been my responsibility to stay on top of his vaccines. So I was right to think that I could never have taken on being a mother. But I used money as an excuse never to have a child. If I had had money, I used to say, I could have afforded a nanny who would have covered for my mistakes.

After Claude was awarded the 40 million (not six million) by the courts, he qualified as the perfect man to take on being a father. Then I began to worry about the child being just another grand Picasso artwork and never having her or his own identity---like Claude.

Tutu's cold body lay on the steel operating table where yesterday he had looked up to me for protection. I had let him down. Failed again. I said a few harsh words to Dr. Miller who had neglected to give Tutu his second Parvo shot, then I kissed Tutu goodbye and left with Heather, in tears. We discussed having an autopsy, but I decided against it. I had been a negligent mother. I was useless. Irresponsible. I had let down the one who loved me the most, just as I felt I had let down Claude and my father. I went home and wanted a drink.

"I'm going to call some of your friends from AA," Heather said. "You need help today, Carole. It wasn't your fault. You did nothing wrong. It was his time. God wanted him. You must accept this."

I remembered the beautiful Irish woman who spoke that night about her dog's death. She didn't cry.

I wanted a pill, a toot, a hit, a snort, a needle, a tall stiff drink.... to fix it.

Then another voice being born in me said, "No you don't. You can do it. Don't blame Tutu for your weaknesses. He didn't complain about his death so why should you? It's your ego to feel this self-pity. He hasn't gone anywhere and neither will you when you die. Put him in your heart and feel his love. You were told you must believe in a higher power, a force greater than yourself to stay sober and to stay alive. Use Tutu. Talk to him every night. Whenever you want. Reach out to that force that put all of us here. Make Super Toots your higher power. Your little lightning bolt. The wings on your spirit. If you believe in him, he can help you believe in yourself. That's what's been wrong with you all these years. If you open your heart to him and let him in, you can fly. He'd want you to. Now that you're sober, you can do anything."

For about a month I had trouble sleeping. I called Billy, another recovering alcoholic, who talked me to sleep night after night. Sometimes until four in the morning. I had to live through this period of my life without drinking or using. This was the toughest period of my sobriety. I was soaking in guilt.

"It's only you doing it to yourself," Billy explained. "Things happen for reasons, though these reasons may not be revealed until much later. Sometimes never at all."

Slowly I became happier, more serene, like I was waking up after a long sleep.

Tutu's death meant my relationship with Claude had finally ended.

I placed a call to Paris wondering who would answer. Claude was in and was alone. For one hour we talked.

"Tutu died, Claude," I said.

"How'd it happen?"

"He didn't get his booster shot of the Parvo vaccine. I think that was the reason, but I'm really not sure."

"It was his time," Claude said. "You'll be fine without him. Get another dog. I did."

"Oh, you did?"

"Absolutely."

"Don't think I could do that." I paused. How could Claude be so heartless? How could he replace Tutu? Maybe he could do it just like he had replaced me. Claude was incapable of a true, lasting love. Then I thought I'd risk it and asked, "How do you feel about me?"

"Of course I still love you, but not in the same way," he said in a murmur. This wasn't what I wanted to hear. But after his suggesting that I get another dog to replace Tutu, it was not a surprise, as it was consistent with the cold and unfaithful character I had seen the last time we met.

I dodged a response. "Claude, guess what I've discovered about myself?"

"You're really a blonde," he said, laughing.

"I'm an alcoholic."

"So that explains it." He was suddenly serious. "That's what happened. Jonas knows a lot about the disease."

"I'm a grateful recovering alcoholic. My sobriety date is December 25, 1980. Recovery is forcing me to take responsibility for things I did and do and to grow up. It's about time. Don't you agree?"

Claude and I laughed like the old days and I could even feel Françoise laughing and Jonas and Paloma while Super Toots barked. It felt good. I felt good.

I forgave Claude for his jilting me as I realized I had been an alcoholic all along, and this had been a huge part of my whole story. He felt relieved knowing this, his guilt assuaged. We were now able to get on with our lives.

Today I have returned home to suburban Philadelphia to teach creative writing at Temple University and Rosemont College. I am able to help young people to cherish their experiences, and to write memoirs about them.

And never to regret the past, but to embrace it by way of the written word.

Acknowledgements

Dr. Catherine Quinn Kerins whose weekly visits I could not do without and whose wisdom guides my every decision. Not to forget Dr. Dante whose kindness nurtured my journey. Mary Dearborn who edited *Picasso's Ghost* and Paul Alexander who believes in my story. Leslie Morris, the Curator of the Houghton Library at Harvard who purchased my Mailer papers and made my publishing this book possible. The gang at Office Depot who helped me upload some thirty photos despite my skills with technology being prehistoric. My niece Audrey Wright who taught me how to upload my cover. Myrna Post who relentlessly has been there for me for every tiny question regarding publicity and who knows her 'stuff'. My French connection, Scott Phillips, who corrected all my French faux pas. Susan Weidener, the creator of The Woman's Writing Circle, who was my inspiration for doing this book and all members of this workshop-- Marie, Diane, Candice, Jan, Mame, Cynthia, Edda, Maureen. The talented artist Frank Batson, my brother-in-law, who urged me to do a drawing of Picasso and still smile. My extended family at the Flourtown Center in Pa. and their relatives in Hollywood who teach me the principles which *Picasso's Ghost* is about. And my facebook friends who have cheered me along the way.